C000051812

Scottish
Bodysnatchers

Norman Adams

GOBLINSHEAD

Musselburgh

Scottish Bodysnatchers

First Published 2002
© Norman Adams 2002

Published by **GOBLINSHEAD**
130B Inveresk Road
Musselburgh EH21 7AY Scotland
tel 0131 665 2894; *fax* 0131 653 6566
email goblinshead@sol.co.uk

British Library Cataloguing in Publication Data
A catalogue record for this book is available from the British Library.

ISBN 1 899874 40 2

Typeset by **GOBLINSHEAD** using Desktop Publishing

If you would like a colour catalogue of our publications please contact:
Goblinshead, 130B Inveresk Road, Musselburgh EH21 7AY, Scotland, UK.

Look out for other related Goblinshead titles on macabre or supernatural topics:

Myth and Magic:
Scotland's Ancient Beliefs and Sacred Places **(£7.50)**

Scottish Witches and Wizards (£5.95)

Haunted Places of Scotland (£7.50)

**Wee Guide to Scottish Ghosts
and Bogles (£3.95)**

**Wee Guide to the Haunted
Castles of Scotland (£3.95)**

Scottish Bodysnatchers

Contents

Acknowledgements

Among the many people who have helped me research the sinister world of the Scottish bodysnatchers my grateful thanks are due to:

Fionna Ashmore, director, Society of Antiquaries of Scotland; Claire Baxter, senior library supervisor, local studies library, Paisley Central Library; Robert Brown, search room archivist, historical search section, The National Archives of Scotland; Miriam Dolby, reference services, National Library of Scotland; George R. Dalgleish, curator, Scottish decorative arts, history & applied art department, National Museums of Scotland; Nancy Davey, Dundee; Jeremy Duncan, library and archives, A.K. Bell Library, Perth; Dr John Fleetwood, senior, Dublin, who has studied the history of the Irish bodysnatchers; Anne Gordon; A.R. Johnston, libraries, information and archives manager, and staff at Ewart Library, Dumfries; Elspeth King, The Smith Art Gallery and Museum, Stirling; Professor M.H. Kaufman, Professor of Anatomy, Edinburgh University; J.M. Pratt, Aberdeen Central Library; Gail Priddice, reference library, Inverness Public Library; the late Ted Ramsey; Ninian Reid; Ian Shepherd, Regional Archaeologist for Aberdeenshire; George Stanley, Rare Books Division, National Library of Scotland; Graeme Wilson, local heritage centre, Moray Council; Alex F. Young, Ayr; Adrian Zealand, heritage programme officer, Dundee City Council; The Editor, The Scots Magazine and staff at City of Aberdeen Public Library, Banchory Public Library and Dundee Public Library.

Introduction

Here lies Nothing.
The impious resurrectionist
At night dared to invade
This quiet spot, and upon it
Successful inroads made
And when to Relatives the fact
Distinctly did appear
The stone was placed to tell the world
There's nothing resting here

(Stone 938, The Howff graveyard, Dundee).
JAMES THOMSON, 'The Book of the Howff'
(Dundee, 1843).

Scots lived and died in fear of them. Bodysnatchers, resurrectionists, sack-'em-up men, shusy-lifters, corp'-lifters or Burkers and Noddies. Call them what you will, but even now their name causes the spine to tingle.

Before the Anatomy Act became law in 1832, the gallows and the poorhouse provided a meagre supply of human corpses for budding young doctors to study anatomy.

There was a burning rivalry between the official colleges and the private schools. Universities teaching anatomy were given priority in the legitimate supply of bodies of condemned criminals and derelicts. But there was never enough fresh bodies to satisfy the demand in both camps and more than one 'subject' brought into the anatomy class bore the stench of the mortcloth, perhaps after a tug-of-war between rival groups.

The so-called golden age of the Scottish resurrectionists took place during the early years of the 19th century when no unguarded grave was spared, and no gravestone left unturned in the quest for 'something for the surgeon'.

Two kinds of resurrectionists prowled burial grounds. On one hand there were the medical students, the amateur bodysnatchers, forced, in some cases, to sell cadavers to their better-off colleagues. And then there were the professionals; the scum of society who brought bodysnatching down to a damnable art. Ella Rodger, whose father joined the 'amateurs' on grave-robbing expeditions in his Aberdeen University days, described the professional resurrectionists as 'human ghouls'.

Victorian writer George MacGregor said the motives of the Resurrection Men were 'not dictated by, and therefore had not the excuse of, a desire for scientific progress, but rather founded on mercenary greed.'

Burke and Hare were devils incarnate. Neither robbed a grave. They murdered for profit, and the revelations of Tanner's Close ensured their place in Scottish folklore.

The stark terror of the general public at that time was described by Aberdeen historian William Buchanan forty years after the resurrectionist panic: 'If any person went home longer than usual they were sure to have been 'Burked'.'

In cities and towns terrified people believed they were under threat from bodysnatchers wielding the dreaded 'pitch-plaster'. This large plaster, coated with a mixture of soft tar and pitch, was used by the 'burker' to suffocate his victim, or so it was said!

Buchanan recalled: 'The hair-breadth escapes from sticking-plasters, and being pursued by doctors, that were retailed each morning were truly wonderful, and timid people were afraid to go out after dark.'

Travelling folk in Aberdeenshire earnestly believed to pass the college gates alone at night risked being hooked around the leg with an iron 'cleik' and dragged inside by medical students. In Glasgow anxious parents warned their offspring not to venture down College Street, although no pedestrian was actually ever 'burked'.

The myth lived on for years after. Young and old hurrying past College Street would clap a hand over their mouths to stifle the effects of chloroform or the pitch-plaster.

But Scots found black humour in the situation. William

Wilson, a Dumfries-shire journalist, wrote in his memoirs how 'Skipper' Henderson, a local character in the village of Sanquhar, was waylaid in a darkened close by jokers brandishing a plaster of strong brown paper covered with treacle. The poor wretch rushed into the first open door sobbing: 'Burkers and plaister!'.

The Scots' belief in the sanctity of the human body was the main reason for their hatred of the bodysnatchers. Their repugnance to dissection was a stumbling block to anatomical research during the first thirty years of the 19th century. Violation of the grave would mean their dear departed would not go to Heaven in a complete state. There were cases where amputees had their severed limb buried long before their own demise.

The bodysnatcher was public enemy number one, and every effort and method was made to protect graves, ranging from a heavy stone slab to a crude land mine, which, thankfully was never put to the test.

An eccentric shepherd, Johnny Turner, also took extreme measures in his choice of a last resting place. His grave was hacked out of solid rock on the summit of Bishop Forest Hill, above Glenkiln Reservoir in Kirkcudbrightshire. Johnny had a dread of the resurrectionists and now lies buried under rock like an Egyptian Pharaoh. He deserves to rest in peace.

Norman Adams, Banchory 2002

Chapter 1
Dawn of the Dead

The ragged beat of the purloined Portsburgh drum sounded a rallying call to an Edinburgh mob hell-bent on mayhem.

Heaven help the chirurgeon or his apprentices who crossed their red-flamed and smoky path.

Their fury was directed at Martin Eccles, a local surgeon, who was suspected of lifting dead bodies, with the help of his band of eager, young apprentices.

Seven days earlier the body of Alexander Baxter had been interred in the burying ground at the hallowed West Kirk (later St Cuthbert's) which, at the beginning of the 18th century, was an isolated place and a soft target for bodysnatchers. The medical men plagued the old kirkyard so often that in 1738 its boundary walls were heightened to eight feet, but the problem refused to go away. The thirst for anatomical knowledge increased the search for human flesh.

Greyfriars Church was another favourite hunting ground for the early Edinburgh bodysnatchers. In May 1711, complaints by the outraged public of rifled graves led to the Incorporation of Surgeons protesting, 'of late there has been a violation of sepulchres in the Greyfriars Churchyard by some who most unchristianly has been stealing, or at least attempting to carry away, the bodies of the dead out of their graves.'

An 88-line Broadside ballad on the scandal was hawked around Scotland.

These monsters of mankind, who made the graves,
To the chirurgions became hyred slaves;
They rais'd the dead again out of the dust,
And sold to them, to satisfy their lust.
As I'm inform'd, the chirurgions did give
Fourty shillings for each one they receive

And they their flesh and bones assunder part,
Which wounds their living friends unto the heart.

In February 1720, Alexander Monro was appointed to the Chair of Anatomy at Edinburgh University. Monro was the founder of a dynasty which spanned 126 years and saw his son and then grandson, both named Alexander, follow in his footsteps with varying degrees of success. The first Monro classes were popular but a lack of raw material from legitimate sources forced student bodysnatchers to step up their activities. Their success can be measured by the fact that in 1721 the College of Surgeons decided that apprentices' indentures include a clause forbidding them to steal bodies. But other professions were less inhibited. In 1753 John Loftas, a grave-digger, was charged with plundering 50 graves and stealing not only coffins and shrouds, but also the fat from corpses.

In 1752, Edinburgh was gripped by wild rumours of apprentice chirurgeons kidnapping citizens for dissection. Monro was forced to move lock, stock and brine barrel after his premises were ransacked.

By 1742, when professional bodysnatchers were supporting the students in supplying fresh corpses, the capital was rocked by serious riots. The trouble began on March 9 with the discovery of Alexander Baxter's body in a house near Eccles' shop.

An enraged crowd gathered outside his premises. They shouted abuse and threatened all surgeons with destruction. The approaching darkness mirrored the mood and the windows of Eccles' shop were smashed. The properties of other surgeons sustained the same treatment.

The magistrates were alerted and the City Guard whose guardhouse stood in the middle of High Street was turned out.

The mob forced the drummer of Portsburgh to surrender his side drum, then beat to arms down the Cowgate, to the foot of Niddry's Wynd, where they were stopped by the City Guard, and the drum wrested from them. (The

Porteous rioters of 1736 were also roused by the tuck of the Portsburgh drum).

The mob nursed their wrath as they melted into the night. But next evening they returned to Eccles' shop, which had a guard at its door. The rioters forced entry and proceeded to demolish its contents. The full weight of the law in the shape of the magistrates, High Constables, and pike-wielding City Guard, managed to disperse the demonstrators. Many of the mob fled by the Netherbow Port, the gate separating the High Street from the Canongate.

The Netherbow and other gates were slammed behind the mob, effectively locking them out of the upper town. The surly protesters broke up.

Mr Eccles and five of his apprentices were cited to stand trial before the magistrates as accessories to the lifting of dead bodies. Eccles and three of his apprentices appeared but the other two fled. However the accused were released because of lack of proof and the charges dropped. (The stigma, it seems, did Eccles no harm. Eleven years later he attended the dying Lady Douglas, a key figure in the protracted Douglas Case, one of Scotland's great civil trials of its kind).

Four days after the riot the Incorporation of Surgeons piously declared their 'abhorrence of so wicked a crime' as bodysnatching. Apprentices were warned they risked losing their indentures if found guilty of having been involved in or having knowledge of dissecting bodies. They faced instant dismissal. Their masters would also be thrown out of the fraternity if implicated in the above violations. A reward of one hundred merks was offered to informants.

But the action failed to soothe the Edinburgh public. On March 15, the mob, fuelled by sinister gossip, were again on the march and no doubt the parishioners of Portsburgh, 'chiefly inhabited by the low order of citizens and mechanics', according to Sir Walter Scott, were in the vanguard.

George Haldane, a beadle at the West Kirk, was suspected

of supplying bodies to the surgeons. The insurgents fell upon his house near the West Kirk. They claimed the two-storey building with garret had been 'built by the gains of the unlawful traffic' of bodysnatching, and promptly nicknamed it, 'Resurrection Hall'. So the term, 'resurrection', as reported in a contemporary account in the *Scots Magazine*, made its ironic debut in the history of bodysnatching. It would soon appear in a slanderous piece of doggerel.

The rioters looted Haldane's house after finding some fragments of old coffins. They stripped the house of booty and returned at nine next morning to wreak further revenge on 'Resurrection Ha''. They systematically dismantled the partitions before setting fire to the debris. All this took place 'without the least opposition' from the authorities.

After reducing the stone walls to rubble, the rioters marched to Grangegateside where they called at the home of another prime suspect, John Samuel, a gardener. Neighbours pleaded with the ring-leaders not to harm the Samuel family or their home and they grudgingly agreed. Before quitting the scene they warned him about his future good conduct. It was a warning he would stupidly ignore, or, as the *Scots Magazine* bluntly reported: 'It seems the love of money made him insensible of his danger.'

Three days after Haldane's house was destroyed, the West Kirk beadle declared his innocence in a public notice in the newspapers: 'All Doctors or Surgeons in Edinburgh or about it, or within the kingdom of Scotland, or any other person that can make it evident that I had any hand or part in lifting the corpses in the West Churchyard, I come in the judges' hands to suffer death.'

Arsonists were busy at Inveresk, four miles east of the capital, on the same day Haldane's declaration was published. A mob entered the home of Peter Richardson, a local gardener, and put it to the torch. He was suspected of being implicated in lifting corpses from Inveresk churchyard, Musselburgh.

But there is no smoke without fire. On March 28 the

common hangman, Jock Dalgleish, who, four years later burnt Bonnie Prince Charlie's standard at Edinburgh Cross, consigned a sedan chair to a bonfire at the same spot. When stopped some weeks earlier at the Netherbow Port, the occupant was found to be a stolen corpse.

John Drummond, chair master, and John Forsyth, chair carrier, told the magistrates they were hoodwinked into transporting the body. The city's chairmen were mainly comprised of fiercely independent Highlanders, whose language was as colourful as their tartan overcoats. The two men's defence was not believed and they were banished.

At the Potterrow Port, on April 6, the 'waiters', the name given to those who guarded the city gates, stopped a man they suspected of carrying prohibited goods. The bag under his arm contained the body of a child, later identified as Gaston, son of Robert Johnston, a Bristo wigmaker. The child's grave at Pentland had been rifled. The man caught red-handed was the same John Samuel who less than a month before had escaped with a grim warning from the fire-raisers who had attacked Haldane's home.

Somehow, Samuel's luck held for he was allowed to go. But word quickly spread and the mob descended on his home at Grangegateside. Samuel had absconded, but he was arrested next day. His wife and bairns were not so fortunate. The contents of their humble home were destroyed, but the mob spared the clothes and bedding of the wretched family out of compassion.

In July 1742 Samuel appeared at the bar of the Court of Justiciary on a charge of violating the sepulchres of the dead. The trial jury found him guilty of being in possession of a dead child but he was cleared of opening the grave. Samuel was sentenced to be whipped through the streets and banished from Scotland for seven years.

The College of Surgeons frowned on such activities, and in 1771 offered a reward for the culprits who abandoned a stolen child's body in a ruined chapel.

In 1749, Glasgow, which would have its full share of resurrectionist scandals in the next century, was rocked by a serious riot when medical students were suspected of stealing bodies from the Ramshorn Kirkyard. The militia was called out but they were unable to prevent injuries and damage to college buildings.

Bodysnatching was not confined to teeming cities with medical schools. In Perth, the town council passed an act in 1724 against the raising of dead bodies from Greyfriars Churchyard, and offered a reward of £10 to anyone who informed. Chirurgeons, if implicated, risked losing their burgess ticket and practice, as well as paying a fine of £20.

Their trainees faced harsher punishment. An extract from the records of Perth Town Council warned: 'Apprentices and others to be fined £5 sterling, whipped and pilloried.' Who were 'the others' who lent their support to grave-robbing? One young man who had recently commenced business as a wright attempted to supplement his earnings by lifting a corpse from Greyfriars. His premises were mobbed but he had already fled town.

His new signboard was torn down and carried in triumph back to Greyfriars where it was hung from a tree close to the violated grave as a warning to other bodysnatchers.

Scotland's tradition in the field of surgery and anatomy went as far back as the early 16th century.

In July 1505, the first charter granted to the Incorporation of Surgeons and Barbers in Edinburgh, made the earliest provision for dissection, whereby every candidate should 'knaw anatomea nature and complexioum of every member in manis bodie.'

In 1657 the surgeons and apothecaries united, and the first maker of surgical instruments in Edinburgh was Paul Martin, a French Protestant refugee, in 1691.

The Edinburgh surgeons were restricted to one felon's body a year until October 1694, when Alexander Monteith, making a bid to open the city's first school of anatomy, was granted 'those bodies that dye in the correction house and of the bodies of fundlings that dye upon the breast.'

Monteith's action stirred other surgeons to secure a grant of 'those bodies that dye in the correction house; the bodies of fundlings who dye betwixt the tyme that they are weaned and thir being put to school or trades; also the dead bodies of such as are stiflet in the birth, which are exposed, and have none to owne them; as also the dead bodies of such as are *felo de se*; likewayes the bodies of such as are put to death by sentence of the magisrat.'

King's College in Aberdeen was founded in 1495 and during its very early years appointed its first 'mediciner', or professor of medicine, well ahead of corresponding professorships in other varsities in Scotland and England.

The earliest medical teaching was based on the classic writings of Aristotle and Galen so instruction in anatomy was rudimentary. In Aberdeen, if human bodies were in short supply, medical students satisfied their curiosity by dissecting dogs and cats.

In 1636, William Gordon, an enlightened mediciner at King's College, petitioned the Privy Council for permission to teach human anatomy, as during the previous two years he had exercised his students in the dissection of animals.

The Privy Council instructed the sheriff and provosts of Aberdeen and Banff to deliver every year to Gordon; 'twa bodies of men, being notable malefactors, executte in thair bonds, especiallie being rebells and outlawis; and failzeing of them, the bodies of the poorer sort, dieing in hospitalls; or abortive bairns, foundlings; or of those of no qualitie, who has died of thare diseases, and hes few friends or acquaintance than can tak exception.'

But Gordon dabbled in politics and failed to establish an anatomical tradition. By 1741 dissections were still being carried out by mediciners in a special room referred to as the Anatomical Hall.

Marischal College, the rival university to King's, was founded in 1593 (they became a single university in 1860), but it did not create a Chair of Medicine until 1700.

The new town became an important centre for medical activity by the close of the 18th century. One reason was the formation of the Aberdeen Medical Society in December 1789 by a group of disgruntled medical students.

But, like their forebears, they had to deal with a shortage of human specimens. Four months after they began the society's minute book bleakly recorded: 'That week a plan for anatomical dissection was put in execution. A dog was dissected.'

In April 1794 a letter advocating bodysnatching was sent to the society by some former members in London.

One of the six signatories was an army surgeon, James McGrigor, who became Director-General of the Army Medical Department for 36 years and is regarded as the founding father of the Royal Army Medical Corps.

The letter read out by Robert Scott, the society's secretary, praised the formative years of the group and its growing reputation.

It ended on a clarion call that clearly incited the medical students to the crime of bodysnatching: 'Above all we would recommend to the Society the study of Anatomy. We are sorry that dissections have been so long neglected at Aberdeen. We are certain that proper subjects might be easily had there and will certainly be unless students are wanting to themselves in spirited exertion or in Common Prudence. Bodies are procured in London for dissection almost every day. We leave everyone to form their own opinion whether it would be not an easier affair at Aberdeen.'

It is no exaggeration to say if the contents of the letter had been made public the reputation of the fledgling society would have been ruined. It is little wonder that members who foolishly leaked proceedings of meetings faced expulsion.

The letter from London fired the enthusiasm of the students, but, in no time at all, they had fallen back into their old habits, with only dogs or a calf's head being dissected. In March 1797 a former member wrote: 'I am persuaded that a subject now and then might be procured in Aberdeen, and much knowledge might be acquired if the inspection of bodies at the hospital was more attended to.'

In 18th-century Glasgow, medical education was available at the university, the private College Street Medical School and Anderson's Institution.

In 1599, the Faculty of Physicians and Surgeons was granted a charter by James VI making it one of the oldest incorporations in the city. The charter was confirmed during the reign of Charles II.

The faculty had the sole power to examine students in medicine and surgery and to grant diplomas, which did not endear itself to the professors at the university. Bitter animosity developed over the years.

In its early years faculty members were exempt from civic duties, such as weapon-training, street patrols, paying tax or jury service.

The groans of the gallows were sweet music to the ears of Scottish anatomists. The 1505 charter of the Edinburgh barber-surgeons, already mentioned, rationed the society once a year to 'ane condampnit man efter he be deid to mak anatomea of, quhairthrow we may have experience ilk ane to instruct uthers, and we sall do suffrage for the soule.'

Because of an apparently botched execution, Scotland can probably claim the dubious distinction of recording the first case of grave-robbing in Britain.

In February 1678 four members of a notorious gypsy family were hanged for murder in Edinburgh's Grassmarket. 'Old Robin' Shaw and three of his sons were convicted of killing 'Old Sandie' Faw, ' a bold and proper fellow', and his pregnant wife in a bloody brawl.

The Shaws and Faws had planned to do battle with bitter rivals, the Browns and the Baillies, at Harestanes in Peeblesshire. Instead they ended up fighting each other.

The executed gypsies were thrown into a pit in Greyfriars Churchyard, and lightly covered with earth. Next morning the youngest, a lad of barely 16, had disappeared. Some observers thought he had revived after a bungled hanging, 'which, if true, he deserves his life, tho' the magistrats, or their bourreau (hangman) deserved a reprimande; but others, more probably, thought his body was stolen away

9

by some chirurgeon, or his servant to make ane anatomicale dissection on: which was criminal to take it at their owne hand, since the magistrats would not have refused it.'

The theory that the gypsy's body was more likely to have been stolen by surgeons strongly suggests that bodysnatching was not unknown at that time in Edinburgh.

Scottish criminal history's most famous uncompleted hanging occurred in 1724 when Maggie Dickson, an inhabitant of Inveresk, was found guilty of concealing the pregnancy of her dead child.

On the Grassmarket scaffold hangman Jock Dalgleish looped the noose around her neck pushed her off the double ladder on which they stood. He swung on her legs for good measure.

After a disgraceful tug-of-war with students over Maggie's apparently lifeless body, her relatives managed to lift her onto a cart and head for home. It was while the mourners stopped for a drink at Peffermill that Maggie regained consciousness because of the jolting of the cart. Her feeble cries brought help. She was fully revived by a surgeon and later allowed her freedom. 'Half-Hangit' Maggie lived for many years and, between adding to her family, earned a living as an ale-house keeper, and a salt crier on the streets of Edinburgh.

A traditional tale from Aberdeenshire had a similar outcome. Merjorie Elphinstone, wife of Walter Innes of Ardtannes, a small estate on the banks of the Don, was roused from her premature burial by a grave-robber attempting to steal the rings from her fingers. Her ornamental tombstone at Inverurie Churchyard gives the date of her death as 1622, but there is no mention of her previous internment. The legend of 'The Goodwife of Kettock's Mill', near Balgownie, Aberdeen, has the miller's wife aroused from her tomb by a grave-robber.

In Chirnside, the minister's wife, Margaret Halcrow, was roused from her coffin by a thieving sexton. Her husband, Rev. Henry Erskine, whom she had wed in 1674, was startled when she knocked on the manse door, imploring:

'Open the door, for I'm fair clemmed wi' the cauld!'

The public went to great lengths to cheat the surgeons of the hanged.

In March 1753 a reputed thief, James Miller, was whipped through Aberdeen streets and banished from the burgh for life.

But his fate was sealed when he was caught red-handed breaking into a house in Inverurie.

On 16 November he was hanged at the Gallowhill, Aberdeen, and his body buried at the gallows's foot. But, according to the *Black Kalendar of Aberdeen*, 'some friendly sailors saved it from the dissecting knife, by soon after taking it up, and carrying it out with them in a yawl, and sinking it in the sea.'

In November 1818, John Barnet was hanged in Aberdeen for theft by housebreaking, after being on the run from jail for a year. His body was buried at sea, but a few days later it came ashore at the mouth of the River Don, and fell into the hands of the surgeons.

After John Worthington was executed at Symington Toll for robbery in 1815, his friends poured vitriol and quicklime into his coffin in the Low Churchyard, Kilmarnock, to render his corpse useless for dissection.

The 'Act for Better Preventing the Horrid Crime of Murder' gave judges the choice of ordering a criminal's corpse to be exhibited in chains – the apparatus resembled a cage of iron – or handed over for dissection. Scottish courts became the first to enforce the act.

In 1779, James McLaughlane, a discharged soldier, murdered Jean Anderson for her cloak, stockings and silver-buckled shoes. He was hanged on Ayr Common and his corpse gibbeted. His body vanished within days. According to local tradition it was removed to protect neighbouring kailyards from the flies attracted to it!

The fate of notorious criminals handed over to surgeons after execution makes abhorrent reading. In 1797, James McKean, a shoemaker, cold-bloodedly murdered and robbed James Buchanan, carrier between Lanark and

Glasgow, after luring the victim to his home in High Street, Glasgow.

McKean's scheme to escape to Ireland became unstuck when his sailing ship was stormbound in Lamlash Bay.

McKean dictated his memoirs in Glasgow Tolbooth before he was hanged at the Cross by Jock Sutherland. His body was given to James Jeffray, professor of anatomy at Glasgow University, who would figure in a controversial 19th-century medical experiment, the result of which reached mythic proportions.

Robert Reid, writing under the pseudonym of 'Sedex' in 1884, gave details of McKean's dissection: 'Some gentlemen in Glasgow anxious to preserve part of the remains of this notorious murderer, asked the doctor to give them the skin of McKean's back, with which request he very obligingly complied. These gentlemen then sent it to a tan-pit to be tanned, and what was very curious, the king's duty was demanded and paid for thus tanning McKean's hide. When the tanning operations were finished, the skin had much the appearance of a common piece of ben-leather. I had a small piece of it in my possession, about the size of a crown piece, and much about the same thickness.'

Thirty-two years later the skin of William Burke, one half of the murdering partnership of bogus bodysnatchers, Burke and Hare, was tanned and cut into portions for the macabre curiosity of public figures.

It is a curious irony that two Edinburgh women pioneered 'burking' 40 years before Burke was born!

Helen Torrance and her upstairs neighbour Jean Waldie spent their wretched lives in a tenement in Fairlie's Close (now New Assembly Close) on the south side of Edinburgh's Royal Mile.

Their victim, John Dallas, a boy of nine, stayed with his parents in Stanielaw's Close (now Stevenlaw's Close), a few steps away from Fairlie's Close.

In November 1751, Torrance offered surgeon apprentices a dead child for sale. The plan hatched by her and Waldie was to substitute the body in its coffin with an equal amount of weight (a ruse worked by Burke and Hare when they sold their first body to Dr Knox). But the mother of the child refused to cooperate and the evil pair turned their attention to wee John, a sickly child.

John's father, John Dallas, senior, a sedan chairman, was at work when his wife, Janet Johnston, visited Torrance, and soon Torrance and Waldie were plying her with booze.

In the course of the false jollity, Waldie slipped down the High Street to Stanielaw's Close. She entered the Dallas house and found the boy alone, and gazing over the window-sill. She gathered the child in her arms and carried him back to her apartment in Fairlie's Close. Torrance later joined her. The kidnapped victim was forced to drink ale and was probably suffocated by Torrance. His thin body was stretched out on a chest of drawers as medical students, unaware foul play had been committed, haggled with the partners in crime over a suitable price.

The students offered two shillings, which the two women grudgingly accepted as part payment of the promised five shillings. Torrance was given an extra ten pence to buy a dram, and received a further sixpence for carrying the corpse to a student's lodgings in the Cowgate in her apron.

A hue and cry panicked the students into dumping the body 'in a place of the town little frequented, with evident marks of it having been in the surgeons' hands.'

At their two-day trial in February 1752 the defence argued that, as the charge did not claim the accused had harmed the child, and selling a dead body was hardly a crime, they should face the lesser evil of kidnapping.

The jury was unimpressed and found: 'That the pannels (the defendants) are both guilty, art and part, of stealing John Dallas, a living child, and son of John Dallas, chairman in Edinburgh, from his father's house, and of carrying him to the house of Jean Waldie, one of the pannels, and soon thereafter, on the evening of the day libelled, of selling and delivering his body, then dead, to some surgeons and students of the physic.'

Torrance delayed sentence by pleading her belly. But she

failed to 'cheat the wuddie' – a medical examination saw to that.

In her final speech from the scaffold, Waldie confessed she had been 'much intoxicated' when persuaded by Torrance to fetch the child. She had believed the boy had been accidentally smothered in her gown-tail. She agreed her sentence was just. Torrance declined to say anything about their crime, but both blamed their predicament on uncleanness and drunkenness.

Scotland's first 'burkers' – mistakenly described as 'Resurrection Women' by Sir Walter Scott – kept their appointment with hangman Jeems Alexander at the Grassmarket on 18 March 1752. Jeems' fee from the council was 10 merks Scots and half-a-crown for the ropes.

The outcome of another 'burking' case, reported in February 1807, is less clear. It took place in Paisley, where Agnes Kelly gave birth to an illegitimate girl, and Matthew Smith, probably the father, offered the child for sale to a 17-year-old surgeon's apprentice for dissection.

Alexander Taylor, arranged to meet Smith in a garden, but when he got there he found the child was not dead. Smith, in Taylor's presence, brutally killed the three-month-old child by squeezing her throat then drowning her in a pond. Taylor took it away and concealed the body, refusing to give any account for it. The men, who were both from Paisley, were accused of abduction and murder. Smith was convicted after trial, but his fate is unknown. Taylor, however, was acquitted, on the basis that presence at the crime, taking away the body and concealing it, were not sufficient to justify a conviction for murder, although Taylor would benefit from the heinous crime.

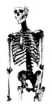

Chapter 2
Doctor's Orders

In the gathering darkness the waters of the Firth of Forth slapped against the rocky foreshore of Fife. The high, rough-stoned walls of Limekilns graveyard loomed above the medical students in a hired row boat as they prepared to steal the body of a drowned sailor.

But out of the gloaming came the sound of weeping. The dead man's fiancee was keeping a lonely vigil. In time she left for home. It was the cue for the students to act. In a twinkling the corpse was inside a sack and on its way to Edinburgh. But as they pulled away the girl returned. Her screams hastened the stroke of their oars as they made their escape. At least one student was wearing a buttonhole of a flower placed by the girl on her sweetheart's grave only a short time before.

The 'snatch' was led by eminent Scots surgeon, Robert Liston, a son of the manse, when he was a pupil at the famous private school of anatomy run by Dr John Barclay.

These amateur bodysnatchers went foraging for fresh corpses far and wide for, unlike England, the theft of the dead had yet to be fully exploited by greedy professionals. Launching a raid across water was much less risky than transporting a stolen body by road.

There was a fisherwife at Anstruther in the East Neuk who, on investigating a suspicious noise at night, looked out to see a stranger bundle a body into a sack and the sack dumped into a boat in the Dreel Burn. Boat, body and bodysnatcher vanished.

On another foray in Fife, Liston, acting on information from a local doctor, set out on a bodysnatching expedition with a colleague disguised as sailors. Their boat was met by the doctor's apprentice who guided them to the graveyard. After the 'snatch' they dumped the body behind a hedge, in a sack, while they went for a refreshment in a local hostelry.

They were flirting with a servant lass when a cry of,

'Ahoy!' was heard outside, and a drunken sailor staggered in carrying the burden the students had left behind the hedge. He heaved the sack on the floor, saying: 'There, if it ain't something good, rot them chaps there who stole it!' He had been slumped behind the hedge when the sack was dumped. The students watched in horror as the sailor cut the sack open to reveal the head of the corpse. The brother and sister fled. Liston hoisted the body onto his powerful shoulders, then he and his colleague headed for the boat with their trophy. They did not stop to pay the bill.

In later years Liston gained the diplomas of the College of Surgeons both in London and Edinburgh, and began practice in Edinburgh in 1818. He also lectured on anatomy and surgery.

Handsome, brilliant and arrogant, Liston had a powerful physique, and strength to match.

His bodysnatching exploits during his teaching years in Edinburgh were legend. On one expedition with his students they had exhumed two of three corpses when their look-out shouted a warning. The air hummed with buckshot as the resurrectionists came under attack from watchers. The snatchers scattered in alarm.

But Liston coolly laid hold of the two large adults bodies, and, carrying one each under the other arm, dashed for a small door in the graveyard wall. He barred the door behind him, and laid low in a private garden until dawn when he slipped away. Later that day porters picked up the 'subjects'.

His formidable strength served him well in the operating theatre where he amputated a limb in 33 seconds: 'The gleam of his knife was followed so instantaneously by the sound of sawing as to make the two actions appear almost simultaneous.'

In Glasgow, too, there were surgeons who led their amateur resurrectionists by example. In 1805, John Burns, founder of the city's College Street Medical School, was banned from teaching anatomy because of his involvement in a bodysnatching case.

His brother, Allan, took over the anatomy class and,

although only 16, performed brilliantly.

In 1809, Granville Sharp Pattison, who would become a colourful and controversial figure in the world of medicine, was appointed Allan's assistant and demonstrator. He also took a leading part in grave-robbing activities.

In evidence to the Select Committee in 1828, Pattison, by then professor of anatomy at the University of London, admitted he had also organised raids while teaching in Glasgow. He would dispatch a group of up to eight students to carry out the work.

A mean passage, Inkle Factory Lane, linked College Street and nearby Ramshorn Churchyard, but the students would range further afield, sometimes with comical results.

After drawing lots two students, acting on a tip-off from a country doctor, headed by gig for the parish of Mearns and the resting place of an 'interesting subject'. They were faced with the problem of smuggling the old man's body past the Gorbals toll-keeper, who was known to have a horrid aversion to bodysnatching.

But the students showed great ingenuity. They dressed the body in an old suit of clothes and a hat they had bought from the Saltmarket and sat it between them on the gig.

One student paid the toll while his companion held up the head of their 'old sick friend' and told him to be of good cheer as they would soon be having breakfast in the High Street. By the glow of his lantern the sympathetic toll-keeper studied the older passenger, then exclaimed: 'O! puir auld bodie, he looks unco ill in the face; drive cannily hame lads – drive cannily.' They got clean away – and on arrival at the medical college they were greeted by their fellow students with a burst of hearty applause.

When Allan Burns died in June 1813 Pattison went into partnership with surgeon Andrew Russel, and together they organised lectures on anatomy and surgery at the College Street Medical School.

But later that year Pattison became involved in a damaging bodysnatching case – the first of several scandals to blight his life.

On 13 December 1813 Janet McGregor, the wife of a Glasgow merchant, Walter McAllaster, was buried in the Ramshorn Kirkyard.

That evening a woman was frightened by a band of students hurrying along Inkle Factory Lane, and next morning the grave was found desecrated. The coffin was exhumed and found to be empty apart from Mrs McAllaster's shroud.

It turned out that resurrectionists had struck twice – a second body had been lifted in the Cathedral graveyard.

In the hue and cry, Mrs McAllaster's brothers accompanied the town's officers on a search of all anatomy rooms in the High Street and Ingram Street areas. It proved grisly work.

Armed with a search warrant they entered Pattison's lecture room where they examined cadavers in various stages of dissection, as well as digging tools. It is no small wonder one brother fainted when he identified his sister's head, disfigured to conceal identity.

Pattison and his students were arrested, and barely escaped lynching from a stone-tossing angry mob as they were taken to the Council Chambers to face further questioning, and eventual release on bail. Pattison was branded a 'shusy-lifter', 'shusy' being the nickname for a pilfered female corpse.

On 6 June 1814, Pattison, his business partner Andrew Russel and students Robert Monro and John McLean, appeared on indictment at the High Court of Justiciary in Edinburgh – the original venue, Glasgow, was objected to by Pattison because of the fear of not getting a fair hearing. The charge was: 'violating the Sepulchres of the Dead.' A move to hold the trial behind closed doors failed but the lordships requested newspaper editors not to publish details that 'would only tend to inflame the minds of the vulgar.'

The defence made great play of the identification of the trunk of a woman's body found in Pattison's lecture room. The body was of a seventeen-year-old virgin, while Mrs McAllaster had been a mother of eight. (A macabre jig-saw of body parts had been completed by the official search party).

After the sixteen-hour long trial Pattison and Monro were found not proven (cynical Scots translate this verdict as 'not guilty – but don't do it again!') while Russel and McLean were found not guilty.

When he gave evidence to the government's Select Committee on Anatomy 15 years later Pattison appeared unrepentant. Asked if the police or magistrates were severe in punishing grave-robbing or looked upon the offence as an unavoidable and necessary evil Pattison replied, 'On the contrary, they behaved with the greatest severity; in my own individual case, the first year I taught there was a skull without teeth found in my dissecting rooms, and because this person had no teeth, I was dragged away by the police, carried through the populace, pelted with stones; I was then indicted, and tried like a common criminal in Edinburgh a man sitting on each side of me with a drawn bayonet.'

'What was the result of the trial?' he was asked. 'An acquittal, which cost me £520,' he replied off-handedly.

In 1816 he was appointed a junior surgeon at Glasgow Royal Infirmary, but he was soon involved in controversy again. A director of the infirmary, Hugh Miller, who was also a senior staff surgeon accused him of unprofessional conduct after two of Pattison's patients died after tricky amputations.

Pattison demanded an inquiry by the infirmary managers, but he and his accuser quarrelled violently at the meeting. The upshot was he challenged Miller to a duel. Miller refused and Pattison labelled him a coward. The unsavoury affair ended with Pattison being censured.

By 1818, Pattison had become Professor of Anatomy and Surgery at Anderson's Institution in Glasgow, while still lecturing at the College Street Medical School.

But his stay at the institution was short-lived. It ended in 1819 after being named the previous year as an adulterer in a sensational divorce action raised by a colleague, Dr Andrew Ure against his wife, Catherine.

ae young Kelvingrove-born surgeon slipped away to United States where he made a worthy contribution to edicine in Baltimore and New York. But controversy was never far behind and eventually he successfully fought a pistol duel with a retired army general. Pattison died in New York on 12 November 1851, aged 60. His body was later reburied in the Glasgow Necropolis.

A month before Dr Ure filed for divorce, he figured in the strange case of Matthew Clydesdale, a miner hanged for murder in Glasgow on 4 November 1818. Clydesdale's corpse was to be dissected by Professor James Jeffray while Dr Ure would demonstrate the effects of electricity on the human body.

Ure attached a voltaic pile (a primitive electrical battery) to Clydesdale. The result was dramatic: Muscles became agitated 'resembling a shudder from cold', and, a lifeless leg shot out with such force that an assistant was almost knocked flying!

The corpse's face twitched in apparent rage, horror, despair and anguish. It flashed ghastly grins. Clydesdale seemed to point a finger at various onlookers, some of whom fled. One man fainted.

But Peter Mackenzie, in *Old Reminiscences of Glasgow and the West of Scotland*, embellished the incident. He claimed Clydesdale returned to life, and rose from the chair on which he had been seated. 'Students screamed out with horror; not a few of them fainted on the spot,' he wrote in his gripping version. 'Dr Jeffray pulled out his unerring lancet and plunged it into the jugular vein of the culprit, who instantly fell down upon the floor like a slaughtered ox on the blow of the butcher!'

Glasgow Cathedral graveyard was a rich source of corpses for the city's amateur resurrectionists. In May 1831 the watch surprised grave-robbers lifting the corpse of John Dempster, a building worker. All of them, except a 19-year-old medical student, John Carmichael, got clean away. His body straddled the graveyard wall when his leg was seized. Carmichael lived across the road from the Cathedral in High

Street, and claimed he had been taking a short cut. He was charged with violating a grave but his case never came to court, probably because the dead man's family were bribed to drop the charge.

Bodysnatchers operated in the Fair City of Perth, where a passageway was known as 'Resurrection Close', because a 'sack-'em-up man' had lived there. A doctor's house in Tay Street had stone steps to the river. It proved a convenient landing place for the delivery of stolen bodies brought across the Tay from graveyards in Kinnoull or Kinfauns. It was whispered the dissecting room was located in the basement of a house.

It could only be reached by a secret staircase within the thick wall. The laboratory was in the attic. It would have suited the notorious Dr Drysdale, patron of Perth bodysnatchers. In 1820 he was implicated in snatching the body of James Taylor, an old retainer of the Earl of Mansfield at Scone. He was dropped from the case. Two other doctors from Edinburgh fled the country and were outlawed by the court.

Anatomists were keen to steal bodies of people with physical deformities. David Ritchie, of Stobo, near Peebles, the sad figure behind Sir Walter Scott's fictional character, The Black Dwarf, had a horror of being dissected. After he died in 1811, it was rumoured he had been snatched by Glasgow resurrectionists. His skeleton was exhumed when a fresh grave was dug. It was reburied but its twisted legs were kept by a local doctor.

The body of an Aberdeenshire dwarf, Alexander Ross, nicknamed, 'Shotty', was eagerly sought by the anatomists. 'Shotty', the tailor at Drumoak on Lower Deeside, was buried in the river-bank kirkyard at Dalmaik. It was feared an attempt would be made to lift his body, and one evening after the funeral a local farmer named Collie saw a strange gig with six men in the vicinity.

Collie rode to nearby Peterculter and broke the news to the village blacksmith, Charles Edward, who set off in hot pursuit on a borrowed horse. When he caught up with the gig four of the medicals were walking in the rear, while two sat in the back with the body in a sack on the floor.

'What have you got in that sack?', demanded Edward.

The enraged blacksmith, muscles bulging, his smoke-blackened face streaked with sweat, presented a fearsome figure, and the bodysnatchers fled into a wood. Edward ripped open the sack with his clasp knife, exposing the bald head of 'Shotty' Ross. The horse and gig were claimed by a horse-hirer in Aberdeen. But by then 'Shotty' had been re-interred.

Aberdeen bookseller Lewis Smith described, in his unpublished memoirs, how the body of his former schoolteacher fell into the clutches of the bodysnatchers. He was five when he attended 'Wiggie' Paterson's school. Paterson earned his amusing nickname because unruly pupils were forced to sit on a stool wearing a wig.

'Wiggie' suffered from knock-knees, a condition highlighted by the fact he wore knee breeches and tight stockings. His school was in Long Acre, a street since demolished, next door to Marischal College, and therefore the schoolteacher would have been a familiar figure to the 'medicals'. 'Wiggie' died in the 1820s, but he did not rest in peace. 'His bones were hung in a glass case in the Anatomical Museum of Marischal College, their identity being proved by the peculiarity of their structure,' wrote Smith.

'Wiggie' was buried in the quaint kirkyard at Banchory-Devenick, the former Kincardineshire parish, within walking distance of the Bridge of Dee in Aberdeen. Because of its close proximity to the town it was a favourite target of medicals despite precautions by anxious parishioners.

In her book, *Aberdeen Doctors*, published in 1898, Ella Hill Burton Rodger, whose father was a 'medical', claimed 'the carriers' cart went in the dusk continually between Banchory-Devenick and Aberdeen with bodies.'

On one notable occasion a party of students belonging to the Aberdeen Medical Society, one of the oldest in Britain, headed for Banchory-Devenick after their lecturer said it was desirable a dead boy should be buried there ' in order that it might be found out what was the matter with him!'

On a frosty moonlight night the young grave robbers, led by 'Long Ned', were defeated at first by the frozen soil. They substituted their shattered spades for the pewter 'bawbee ladles' they took from the vestry. They had no sooner lifted the body when a group of angry locals showed up. The students fled, but when they reached the Bridge of Dee their way was barred by townsfolk.

'Long Ned' was urged to drop the sack into an ice hole. His aim was erratic and it plunged into the river, where it was rescued. The incident soured relations between town and gown and forced one student, who later became a prominent doctor in Peterhead, to keep a low profile at his uncle's home on Ythanside.

In 1813, three medical students were arrested after a 'stiff tussle' with relatives of the deceased who were keeping watch. They were taken before the Sheriff at Stonehaven and committed to prison on charges of attempting to steal the body, and for assaulting the watchers. They were found guilty after trial and ordered to pay a fine of £20, most of which was donated to the poor of the parish of Banchory-Devenick.

The minutes of the Aberdeen Medical Society from 1806 to 1808 give a fascinating glimpse of the bodysnatching activities of its members.

Each student had to take his turn in watching the town's churchyards, including the Spital (now part of St Peter's) and St Machar's Cathedral in Old Aberdeen. Those who refused were fined and the money shared between those who kept watch. The amateur bodysnatchers were paid ten shillings and sixpence each (52.5p) for lifting a 'subject'. The pay was later increased, plus an additional one shilling (5p) 'to warm the insides of their jackets.'

In those early years many meetings were postponed because members were otherwise engaged dissecting a fresh 'subject'.

Here is a typical entry, dated 12 November 1805: 'Messrs.

Officer, Davidson, J. Gordon, and Rankine intimated to the members that they had procured a subject from the old Town Churchyard and which was safely lodged in the Anatomical theatre. Dr Skene was to take the trouble of undertaking the dissection. It is hoped that the exertions of the above will prove a stimulus to the rest of the members.'

The minute of 23 February 1806 records the following calamity: 'Some of the members having procured a subject lodged it in the Society's Hall, where in the course of the same day it was unfortunately discovered. At night the body was returned to the Spittal burial-ground, from which it had been taken.'

Dr William Livingstone, the Society's first honorary president, was forced 'for prudential reasons' to evict members from their premises.

They moved their library, museum, and meeting place to Dr Skene's classroom, but Dr Livingstone promised he would be among the first subscribers to a more permanent home.

Meanwhile Sheriff Dauney mildly rebuked the Society and imposed a collective fine of one guinea which Mr Burnett, procurator-fiscal, promptly remitted.

But that was not the end of the affair. The dead man's widow called on Dauney and said his brothers had kept details of the outcome of the case from her, and believed they had been paid off. The Sheriff advised the Society that the guinea fine which the procurator-fiscal had not exacted should be given to her 'to stop her clamour'.

But there had been trouble of a less serious nature in earlier times. In 1800, one member was allowed to resign on threat of expulsion, for repeatedly divulging the secrets of the Society, 'particularly by informing Mr Hector's servant-maids of the transactions at times of dissections.'

In 1808 three members were accused of stealing a body from the Society's rooms. It was eventually found in an adjoining room!

One bodysnatching exploit not recorded in the Society's

Minutes concerned the theft of the corpse of James Marr, a miller, from the Spital Churchyard, in October 1801. The body had been stolen by Charles Jameson, and unnamed accomplices, twelve days before Jameson was appointed the Society's Secretary!

A well-kent character in resurrection times in Aberdeen was George Pirie, the sacrist of Marischal College, who witnessed the trust deed with the Aberdeen Medical Society.

He was paid to help rob the graves and to act as a 'minder' if events turned nasty.

Bodysnatching was rife elsewhere in North-east Scotland.

In 1817, three apprentices to a local surgeon, John Gordon, were accused of violating the sepulchre of the dead by lifting the newly-interred body of John Bremner at Keith, Banffshire.

James Taylor, John Gordon and George Pirie were fined guilty after trial at the Spring Circuit Court in Aberdeen, but the jury appealed for clemency because of their youth. The accused also offered to pay compensation to the dead man's family. The good folk of Keith had also been moved to petition the court for a lenient sentence. The Lords Pitmilly and Reston locked up the accused for four months.

The theft of the body of 90-year-old Mrs Janet Spark from St Fittick's in Torry, Aberdeen, in December 1808 had a macabre outcome. Mrs Spark, the widow of an Aberdeen shipmaster, was ferried across the Dee to be buried in the tiny kirkyard which overlooks the Bay of Nigg. The mourners failed to notice the two young men who accompanied them on the short hop.

That night the two men were disturbed by the barking and approach of the minister's dog from the manse next door to the graveyard. Next morning there was a gaping hole in the ground. The coffin had been crudely opened and broken pieces lay scattered around with remnants of the shroud. There were traces of blood on the coffin lid, and a vital clue: a spade with the name 'Rae' carved on the handle.

On a dreary day in February 1809 Mrs Spark's nude

body unexpectedly turned up – washed ashore on the bay!

The students, when arrested, said they had decided not to transport the body back to Aberdeen because of the risk factor. Instead they had buried it in a bank of sand at the Bay of Nigg.

Before they could retrieve the corpse a great storm battered the region and carried off the late Mrs Spark.

At the February session meeting the minister reported, 'that the person principally concerned in taking up the body was found to be a forward, impudent, not well-behaved young man, a student in physic, who had been obliged to flee from the country.' The abandoned spade had belonged to his father, who had to pay Mrs Spark's family compensation.

The zealous activities of the amateur resurrectionists could become farcical. A horror-struck minister found an abandoned body in sack in an outhouse of the manse garden at Bieldside, a suburb of present-day Aberdeen. A student was foolish enough to hide a body in a flour sack in his father's bakery, ruining trade.

Rumours spread in Old Aberdeen that a house was haunted. Spectral figures in shrouds flitted in and out of the property. Of course, the rumours were put about by medical students who used the premises as a short cut to and from local burial grounds.

In Aberdeen, Dr Andrew Moir, born of humble parents in 1806, earned high praise as a brilliant anatomist during his short life. He was earmarked for a religious career but before choosing medicine he mingled his two studies, studying anatomy at Marischal College and divinity at King's College. Moir and his colleagues struggled under the heavy burden of incompetent medical lecturers, a hostile public and rivalry of inter-varsity factions. In later years he would describe medical lectures as a 'mere sham', with one lecturer giving only three in one year. Moir was said to have been 'the chief support of the anatomical class in the College', which guardedly meant that he was a most active bodysnatcher, for in those early days 'the poorer pupils frequently procured bodies, not only for the lecturer, but for the purpose of sale to their more unfortunate brethren.' After taking the diploma of the Royal College of Surgeons of England in 1828, he applied to join the army. But there was no vacancy so he returned to Aberdeen, after a fleeting visit to Paris where he was fascinated by The Morgue, with its endless supplies of dead bodies drowned in the Seine or found in the streets.

When he set out for London the doctor carried glowing testimonials from his university professors. But on his return they savaged him when he announced plans to become an extra-mural lecturer. He was stigmatised as a 'worthless character and as a common resurrectionist, unfit for the society of gentlemen'. They called him 'clever, dirty Andrew Moir' behind his back. Moir was forced to do his own chores. He even led bodysnatching raids

On one outing Moir jammed his hand under the coffin lid while standing in the open grave. 'Heave down the earth, my lads,' he called cheerfully to his students. It was rumoured he led a raiding party on his minister brother's own kirkyard. Moir insisted every member of his class took a turn in stealing bodies. Anyone who absented himself from depositing or digging up a dead body faced a fine of ten shillings and sixpence, unless indisposed. Students who refused to exhume a body without a reasonable excuse were excluded. The fines were divided among the class.

The bodysnatcher slur made sure that few, if any, private patients knocked on Moir's door. It was said he was almost as penniless as his students. But Moir persevered and the Aberdeen anatomist built up an unsurpassed knowledge of anatomy. His former students performed with great distinction in the south, and Moir earned high praise from Sir Astley Cooper. But, as we shall see, the Burke and Hare outrage would bring anatomists such as Andrew Moir into even greater disrepute.

The demand for fresh bodies never flagged. But as the public became better informed so tougher measures were introduced to baulk the bodysnatchers. The price of bodies rose, and anatomists, particularly those in Edinburgh, were reduced to supplying themselves from London and elsewhere.

At that time, Dr Monro, of Monro dynasty fame, and Liston's former lecturer, Dr John Barclay, had avoided confrontation by acquiring bodies from their agreed territories in and around the capital. But, with Liston back on the scene in 1818, that cosy arrangement would be blown apart, and a new breed of resurrectionist made his appearance on the Scottish scene.

Chapter 3
The Specialists

They were the odd couple of Scottish bodysnatching.

Liston, a future Professor of Clinical Surgery in University College, London, teamed up with Ben Crouch, a retired London professional resurrectionist, known as the 'Corpse-King'.

Their paths had crossed in London and in 1818 the obnoxious Crouch, bully, ex-pugilist, and flash dresser, was taken on Liston's pay roll as an instructor, after he fled to Edinburgh on being released from jail for assault.

Crouch, son of a carpenter at Guy's Hospital, London, was introduced into the bodysnatching business by Sir Astley Cooper (1768-1841), a noted surgeon and a patron of the resurrectionists of London. In 1820 he ordered that the body of a man on whom he had operated the previous day was to be obtained, 'cost what it may.'

His opinion of Crouch and his kind was expressed at the hearing of Select Committee on Anatomy in 1828: He described them as the 'lowest dregs of degradation'. He added: 'I do not know that I can describe them better; there is no crime they would not commit, and, as to myself, if they should imagine that I would make a good subject, they really would not have the smallest scruple, if they could do the thing undiscovered, to make a subject of me.'

Be that as it may. Liston and Crouch formed a fruitful partnership. Their most notorious exploit was uplifting the body of a country lad with a hydrocephalic head who was buried by the Firth of Forth.

The graveyard look-out resisted bribes of cash and whisky from prowling bodysnatchers. The agents of Monro and Barclay were willing to part with large sums to obtain the 'rare osteological specimen', but to no avail.

The clamour had all but died down when 'two well-dressed gentlemen, smoking their cigars', rolled up in a dog-cart at the local inn early one evening. The 'whip-hand' told the ostler that he expected a livery servant to bring a parcel for him.

The two 'dog-cart' men went for a walk, but they had not gone half-an-hour when the servant in scarlet livery turned up with the parcel. He locked it in the boot, then left. Shortly afterwards, the two gentlemen returned and drove off in the direction of Edinburgh. When the watch reported for duty they soon discovered they were guarding an empty grave. They made for the inn when word circulated about the 'dog-cart' men. It was then the ostler remembered he had caught the flash of red under the overcoat of one of the gentlemen as he boarded the vehicle. He also recalled that the servant who had locked away the parcel had slipped the key into his pocket. The 'whip-hand' man was Liston. Crouch was his companion.

In less than half-an-hour, in daylight, or at best in gathering dusk, they had robbed a grave that had beaten their rivals. The outrage sparked off a hunt for the impudent bodysnatchers. The parish minister and dominie hurried to Edinburgh where they were invited to search the premises of Monro and Barclay. The crest-fallen hunters rode home and a rare anatomical specimen remained in the capital. The skeleton was donated by Liston to the College of Surgeons.

When Liston gate-crashed the Edinburgh bodysnatching scene the gentleman's agreement between Monro and Barclay about the sharing of spoils ended. Fist fights between rival bands of medical students became commonplace in the graveyard.

When a lame street singer, Sandy McNab, died in the Infirmary, Dr Cullen and his students placed the body in a box and prepared to hoist it by ropes to their rooms above. A rival group of Monro's students showed up and began lifting the box over the wall. A brawl ended with the attackers fleeing empty handed.

Sir Robert Christison described a graveyard fracas which saw Liston and Crouch give ground to their rivals.

He explained: 'It was no uncommon occurrence for one party to have a look-out man sitting on the churchyard wall in the dangerous dusk, ready to drop down on the first appearance of the rival party, and appropriate the grave by striding across it. My hospital comrade, Mowbray Thomson, had a risky encounter in this way. Though his assistantship with Dr Barclay's necessarily ceased on his becoming an Infirmary resident, he had so great a passion for adventure, that he used to drop from his window, scale the city wall which then bounded the hospital grounds to the south, and join his former companions in their unholy occupation. On the occasion referred to, he was perched on the churchyard wall as sentinel, when Liston hove in sight with his assistants, and a notorious London resurrectionist, Crouch, who had made the metropolis too hot for him, and had been taken into Liston's pay as an instructor during his rustication in Edinburgh.'

Christison went on: 'Thomson jumped into the burying ground, sat down across the grave, stuck his digger into it, and when the intruders followed him, claimed the grave as his. Liston and Crouch first jeered him, and then threatened to remove him by force. But, as they drew near for the purpose, he presented a pistol in the face of the foremost, and swore he would defend himself to the uttermost. More altercation ensued, during which succour to the weaker party arrived in the shape of Thomson's companions. A general row appeared imminent; but Liston thought better of it, and left the enemy in undisturbed possession of their claim.'

Crouch had been a member of a large London gang but it broke up after he demanded they charge surgeons more for bodies. He later had the sole supply of 'subjects' to most of the anatomical establishments in London, and was therefore in a position to demand a higher price. He died a pauper in London.

Speculation can be made on the reasons behind a string of anonymous letters to the authorities about impending raids by professional resurrectionists in the Lothians and Fife. Perhaps the motives of the letter writer or writers were to get rid of the opposition then create a monopoly in price-fixing.

In January 1819, Catherine Mack was buried in the quaint kirkyard at Prestonkirk, east of Edinburgh. The next day Mr Gibb, the postmaster at Linton, now East Linton, received an anonymous warning that an attempt would be made to lift her body. He assisted constable Ralph Plain and two village lads, all armed with firearms, to catch three Edinburgh men red-handed. The culprits were each jailed for one year.

In the opening months of 1820 a gang of professional bodysnatchers was kept busy on both sides of the Forth, raiding graves at Kirkliston, Abercorn and Scotlandwell, Fife.

Acting on another anonymous letter, two nephews of James Fisher, whose body was lifted from Scotlandwell in March, were accompanied by a court officer on a search of the anatomy school run by Dr Lazzar in Surgeons' Square.

There was no sign of the missing body until the doctor reluctantly pulled a lever to reveal a secret vault under the hearth stone. It was occupied by Fisher's partly-dissected body.

Dr Lazzar's gang comprised of six persons, five of whom were professional snatchers. Despite the mass of evidence the Lord Advocate decided not to prosecute. One of the gang was probably Daniel Butler, an articulator and dealer in bones, a former member of the Ben Crouch gang in London. He was later sentenced to death for a mail-coach robbery in Edinburgh, but reprieved.

One of Edinburgh's weirdest gang was headed by Andrew Merrilees, commonly known as 'Merry Andrew', a tall, gaunt human scarecrow with 'jaws like an ogre' who jerked like a puppet as he walked, his long pale face twitching.

The former carter's bodysnatching activities in the country (his house overlooked a graveyard) forced him to flee.

His associates were 'Spune' (Spoon), 'Mowdiewarp' (Mole), Mowatt, who earned his sobriquet because of his digging ability. Spune, who had the look of a broken-down parson, was nicknamed after his spoon-shaped spade. Mowatt took up bodysnatching when he failed as a plasterer.

Merrilees sometimes called on the services of 'Praying Howard' , who in bible black suit and white choker, would impersonate a clergyman at funerals, while noting the lay-out of the graveyard. Another associate was dubbed, 'Stupe'.

They proved an efficient team, when not trying to swindle each other. Merrilees was accused of cheating 'Spune' and Mowatt out of ten shillings (50p) when dividing their fee from the doctors.

By chance, a sister of Merrilees died in Penicuik, and her grasping brother saw an opportunity to make money. He did not involve his sulking associates in his cold-hearted plan, but they knew something was afoot when they spotted him wearing mourning clothes. They hatched a plan to lift Merrilees' sister, and sell her to the doctors.

They hired a donkey and cart to bring the body back to Edinburgh. But their crafty boss had learned of their intentions from the man who had hired the cart to Spune and Mowatt.

At Penicuik, the two bodysnatchers swooped on the unguarded grave. Merrilees, carrying a white sheet, hid behind a tombstone. He bided his time till they had lifted the corpse. Then, with an eerie yell, an apparition rose from behind a tombstone, and put them to flight. 'The Spune maun dae withoot its porritch this time,' chortled Merrilees. 'And shall not maun live on the fruit of the earth?'

Merrilees shouldered his sister's body then made for home. On the darkened road ahead of him Spune and Mowatt led the donkey and cart away. Startled by a loud shout at their backs they abandoned their transport and took to their heels.

Merrilees dropped his bundle in the cart, and set off for Surgeons' Square, to collect £10 and more for a 'subject'

A figure of ridicule to the medical students, Merry Andrew himself was famously deceived as he loitered at a close mouth, waiting for the demise of an old woman. A voice belonging to a shadowy student whispered in his ear:

'She's dead.'

Merrilees barged into the humble dwelling and called out to the old crone who acted as the invalid's nurse: 'It's a' owre I hear. And when will we come for the body?'

'Whisht, ye mongrel,' growled the nurse, 'She's as lively as a cricket.'

The terrified invalid overheard the ominous conversation and died next day. Merrilees and Spune returned with tanner's bark to substitute for the body in the coffin, but the nurse had second thoughts.

'A light has come doun upon me frae heaven, an' I canna.' Snorted Merrilees: 'Light frae heaven! Will that shew the doctors how to cut a cancer out o' ye, ye auld fule?'

'But we'll sune put out that light,' he whispered to his companion. 'Awa' and bring in a half-mutchkin.' Before he went off to buy whisky, Spune remarked, 'Ay, we are only obeying the will of God. Man's infirmities shall verily be cured by the light o' His wisdom. I forget the text.'

Merrilees, filling the nurse's glass, told her, 'Tak' ye that, and it will drive the deevil out o' ye.'

After she had drained a second glass the bodysnatcher held a pound note up to a guttering candle and said: 'And noo, look through it, ye auld deevil, and ye'll see some o' the real light o' heaven that will mak your cat's een reel.'

The nurse wavered. But would not be cheated out of her rightful reward. 'But that's only ane,' she whined, 'and ye ken ye promised three.' 'And here they are,' replied Merrilees.

'Weel, ye may tak her.' But at that moment a stranger, dressed in a greatcoat, wide cravat with a broad bonnet concealing his face, entered. He announced he was the dead woman's nephew, and wanted to view the body. A not-so-merry Andrew and Spune slipped out of the house, followed by the stranger who pretended to give chase. He was, of course, the student who had been behind the prank from the beginning. The dead woman was decently buried, although another version of the tale saw the students snatch the corpse. Either way the nurse was three pounds richer.

Merrilees did business with Dr Robert Knox, and on the eve of the Burke and Hare murder revelations, the surgeon's handyman, Davie Paterson, paid the resurrectionist in advance for a 'subject'. In October 1828 Merrilees had delivered the following note:

'Doctor am in the east, and has ben doin little busnis, am short of siller send out abot aught and twenty shilins way the carer the thing will bee in abot 4 on Saturday mornin its a shusa, hae the plase open. And. M———s.' But the crafty Merrilees never delivered the woman's corpse. Paterson discovered he had sold it to another doctor.

So much for the murkier doings of Edinburgh's professional resurrectionists.

In Glasgow, it was mostly the medical students themselves who lifted bodies, although 'subjects' were supplied by professionals, such as Henry Gilles, a former gravedigger, sacked after he resold grave furniture to undertakers.

Gilles later alarmed the good folk of Anderston, where the villagers had clubbed together to buy land for their own private graveyard. Mourners complained he was measuring the depth of graves with a sharp-pointed cane.

In the early hours of St Patrick's Day 1828, Gilles was in a gang chased by police after dumping two bodies in North Street, Glasgow. The bodies of an old woman and a child had been lifted at Anderston. Gilles' fate is unknown.

Outside of Edinburgh no other Scottish town or city had large gangs of professional resurrectionists roaming local graveyards. Unscrupulous grave-diggers were known to make ready cash by passing on information to 'medicals' about impending funerals. They also stooped to plunder graves.

In Aberdeenshire, the grave-digger at Newhills, commonly known as 'Resurrectionist Marr', was rumoured to have worked for several years with Peter Brownie, a young farmer from Fintray, who converted to Quakerism. Brownie died in 1886.

In Aberdeen, in the early 19th century, James Sangster,

a watchman in the Gallowgate, was rumoured to lift bodies from the Spital graveyard. He sold his wife's body to the anatomists, and was known until his death as 'Satan'. In 1832, an Ayr carter, 'Burke' Morrow, earned his detestable nickname after he was suspected of transporting body parts.

A grave-digger was immortalised in an old street ballad, *The Roond-Moo'ed Spade*. Geordie Mill, the sexton of Dundee, was suspected of stealing bodies from The Howff, where many victims of the city's 1832 cholera epidemic lie buried.

The ballad tells how Geordie took delivery of a 'hairy trunk' sent by Leith steamer by a doctor. Inside were nine sovereigns, 'The price o' a well-fed, sonsie quine they had sent to Monro ae mornin'', and a note from the doctor ordering 'a double doze by the coach on Wednesday mornin''.

Geordie hurried off to inform his accomplices, Robbie Begg, and Tam and Jack, 'the lads that used the spade an' pock.' A dram fortified the snatchers as they made plans to lift a body, despite a warning from Robbie's wife. But events went awry as:

'The hour grew late, the tryst was lain
Amang these Resurrection men,
When each his glass did freely drain,
Sayin', 'Here's success to the mornin''.'

'But Robbie noo does sair repent
His slightin' o' the warnin' sent,
For the noise o' a second coffin's rent
Caused in Dundee a deil o' a mornin''.'

Mill's neighbour, William McNab, a weaver who was a 'watcher o' the dead' during resurrectionist times, was suspected of penning the scurrilous ballad. He was questioned by magistrates but cleared. Mill was suspended probably because of the unwelcome publicity.

A glance at the criminal records suggest resurrectionists

escaped harsh punishment. Many cases never got the length of a court. But one habitual bodysnatcher received one of the toughest sentences handed down to his breed.

In March 1823, a farmer rode to Linlithgow to raise the alarm after a servant spotted two men dig bundles out of a dung heap. The gig was stopped in the town and the lone driver dragged to the ground by a crowd and badly beaten. Three corpses were found in the gig, one of which was of a child, a miner's daughter, who had been buried at Larbert. The bodysnatcher gave a false name but he was identified as Thomas Hodge, of Edinburgh. Hodge refused to divulge the name of his accomplice. At the High Court in Edinburgh he probably regretted his silence, for he was transported to Australia for seven years.

In 1829, as the country reeled from the Burke and Hare revelations, and Burke's execution, Helen Begbie, a young Midlothian widow, became the first woman in Scotland to have joined in a bodysnatching raid.

The she-devil had been married to a bodysnatcher jailed for the theft of bodies at Lanark. She kept herself in drink by selling information on recent burials to resurrectionists.

Helen passed on details of several funerals in the village of Lasswade, near Edinburgh, where she herself stayed. Three bodies – a man, woman and a child – were lifted. The man was Helen Begbie's cousin.

The bodies of the two adults were sold to doctors in Surgeons' Square. One buyer, Dr Lazzar, whom we have already met, purchased one for 10 guineas and promptly sold it to a colleague for a five guinea profit.

The Sheriff Officer and his men eventually rounded up the gang, but only three members were convicted and jailed. John Kerr, a persistent bodysnatcher, was given nine months' hard labour. Helen was never brought to justice.

So what dark secrets lay behind the 'roond-moo'ed' spades and other such paraphernalia of the Scottish bodysnatchers?

Chapter 4
Here Today, Gone Tomorrow

'I'll never forget it,' wrote a horrified Mansie Wauch, on finding that the graves of the town kirkyard had been violated by bodysnatchers.

The eponymous hero of D. M. Moir's fictional autobiography described the outrage and misery of the good folk of Dalkeith.

'I was standing by when three young lads took shools (shovels), and, lifting up the truff (turf), proceeded to houk down to the coffin, wherein they had laid the grey hairs of their mother. They looked wild and bewildered like, and the glance of their een was like that of folk out of a madhouse; and none dared in the world to have spoken to them. They did not even speak to one another; but wrought on with a great hurry, till the spades struck on the coffin-lid – which was broken. The dead-clothes were there huddled together in a nook, but the dead was gone. I took hold of Willie Walker's arm, and looked down. There was a cold sweat all over me; – losh me! but I was terribly frighted and eerie. Three more graves were opened, and all just alike, save and except that of a wee unchristened wean, which was off bodily, coffin and all.'

The Life of Mansie Wauch, Tailor in Dalkeith: Written by Himself, originally appeared in magazine form in 1824. David Macbeth Moir (1798-1851), a Musselburgh man, received his surgeon's diploma at Edinburgh University at the age of 18, and would have been acquainted with the activities of the resurrectionists.

The exhumation methods of the bodysnatchers remained a mystery for many years. Even now it is probable that some of their unholy secrets died with them.

The speed with which corpses were stolen was incredible, and if the bodysnatchers went undisturbed they usually left behind no evidence of their crime. The general public relied on writers of fiction to explain how the 'sack-'em-ups' operated. In his classic tale of terror, *The Body-Snatcher*, Robert Louis Stevenson describes how Fettes and Macfarlane uncovered a coffin at Glencorse before heaving it to the surface. In *A Tale of Two Cities*, Dickens erroneously has Jerry Cruncher and his associates wrenching a coffin from a grave with the aid of a gimlet (oddly, an anecdote of bodysnatching in Edinburgh claims the snatcher was nicknamed, 'Screw', while a 'resurrection screw' serves as a bolt on the lychgate of a Devon churchyard).

If the resurrectionists were inexperienced, or in a hurry to leave, they left behind an atmosphere of terror, misery, and desecration for all to see. In September 1823, an Edinburgh newspaper horrified its readers with the report of grave-robbing at Crichton, Midlothian: 'The body of a young man of most respectable parents belonging to Stobhill had been decently interred on Thursday prior, in a grave 13-feet deep. The grave, on the morning of Saturday was found open; the coffin broken to pieces; the linen torn and strewn about, and, instead of the body, a large swarm of black maggot flies, which the unwholesome air had attracted to the spot. The parents, as might be expected, were almost inconsolable on hearing of this horrible robbery.'

But with time on their side the bodysnatchers restored the grave to its original condition. This was not done out of compassion, but as an elaborate precaution against discovery, so that they could return to the graveyard again. If local inhabitants did not suspect their kirkyard had been desecrated they would lower their guard, or, perhaps even not bother to mount a watch.

But such trickery by the resurrectionists sometimes failed.

In January 1816, the keen eye of a countryman on his way to worship at Ormiston, near Haddington, noticed that his friend's grave had been disturbed. A local stone mason, William Todd, had been buried five days earlier. But Simon Notman, on inspecting the grave, noticed the earth had been disturbed. There was too much bottom soil visible. The coffin was exhumed. It was found to be in perfect condition with no evidence of it having been tampered with.

But when the grave-digger opened the lid the coffin was empty.

Three medical men, the sons of a wealthy local farmer, were the culprits, but they escaped punishment. Alexander Wright, the eldest, served as a surgeon with the Edinburgh Militia. He fled to the South Atlantic on a naval ship. His brothers, David, a doctor in Edinburgh, and Andrew, a medical student, refused to answer questions. Todd's body had been hidden in an outhouse before it was smuggled to an anatomist. It was never recovered. Bodysnatching was a seasonal occupation. The robbers operated in winter but not on moonlight nights. A bright moon would make their activities impossible.

According to Christison: 'The time chosen in the dark winter nights was, for the town churchyards, from six to eight o'clock; at which latter hour the churchyard watch was set, and the city police also commenced their night rounds.'

Operations in country parishes were conducted at a later hour, he added. 'Certain country churchyards were selected for the convenience of approach, and their distance from houses. Although there was more risk in such circumstances, owing to the necessity of using a gig, and the inquiries that were apt to take place at toll-bars, no one was ever caught. But narrow escapes were sometimes made.'

The tools of their trade included a lantern, grapnels, sacks, crowbar, a sheet of canvas, a pickaxe, perhaps, and, most importantly, spades. No common or garden spade was used. Professional resurrectionists would sometimes be armed with a pocket pistol. If a kirkyard wall proved an obstacle a collapsible ladder was useful. They might even wear special clothing because clay clung to their clothes and boots. Smocks were worn, and faces blackened to avoid recognition. 'Things' for the surgeon were usually packed in a roped tea-box, or even an old carpet.

At Coull, three miles north of Aboyne, Aberdeenshire, where there is a turf-roofed mort-house, a watch was mounted after some graves were tampered with. The bodysnatchers were caught red-handed and were badly mauled. One young doctor was said to have been so badly injured he never fully recovered. The grave-digger vanished from the district. However, none of the snatchers were arrested but they did leave behind a pickaxe, spade, screwdriver and a telescopic pole with a hook on the end. It was thought this instrument was intended either to lift the coffin or drag out the body. These artefacts were preserved for a time but have since been lost. The Coull resurrectionist wasn't the only 'medical' to be maimed in North- east Scotland. Dr Macpherson of Aberlour was handicapped with a stiff arm as a result of an encounter with watchers. He and a fellow student had succeeded in snatching a body when their gig was set upon.

So how was a body 'resurrected'? Bransby Cooper, nephew and biographer of Sir Astley, remarked on the speed bodies were snatched (at Kirkmichael, Ayrshire, in March 1829, 22 bodies were found to have vanished over a short time span), 'but the means by which it was accomplished was one of the mysteries of their occupation. This was never fathomed by the public, and curiously enough, no accidental circumstances occurred to furnish the solution.'

Henry Lonsdale, the devoted pupil and assistant of that much maligned Edinburgh anatomist, Dr Robert Knox, whose career would be ruined by the Burke and Hare scandal, described one particular method.

He wrote: 'In the disinterment of bodies considerable force was required, and this was mainly exerted round the neck by means of a cord and other appliances. Now, withdrawing the contents of a coffin by a narrow aperture was by no means an easy process, particularly at dead of night and whilst the actors were in a state of trepidation; a jerking movement is said to have been more effective than violent dragging.'

Thomas Wakley, the founder of the medical journal, *Lancet*, published an improbable version of stealing a body in 1823. It involved grave-robbers digging a narrow tunnel from a distance of 15 or 20 feet away from the head or foot of the grave. The rough, slanting shaft would have had to impinge exactly on the coffin, which was then heaved up by hooks to the surface, or preferably, its end wrenched off with hooks while still in the shelter of the tunnel. The scalp or feet of the corpse was secured through the open end, and the body pulled out, leaving the coffin almost intact and unmoved. The body once lifted, the shaft was filled in. A bodysnatcher would have had to crawl into the tunnel to wrench off the coffin lid, before his accomplices attempted to pull it or the body up to the surface. No mean task.

Sir Robert Christison's memoirs, edited by his sons, give the most accurate account of the unhallowed art:

'A hole was dug down to the coffin only where the head lay – a canvas sheet being stretched around to receive the earth, and to prevent any of it spoiling the smooth uniformity of the grass. The digging was done with short, flat, dagger-shaped implements of wood, to avoid the clicking noise of iron striking stones.'

Christison, who either witnessed or took part in bodysnatching raids, continued: 'On reaching the coffin, two broad iron hooks under the lid, pulled forcibly up with a rope, broke off a sufficient portion of the lid to allow the body to be dragged out; and sacking was heaped over the whole to deaden the sound of the cracking wood. The body was stripped of the grave-clothes, which were scrupulously buried again; it was secured in a sack; and the surface of the ground was carefully restored to its original condition, – which was not difficult, as the sod over a fresh-filled grave must always present signs of recent disturbance. The whole process could be completed in an hour, even though the grave might be six feet deep, because the soil was loose, and the digging was done impetuously by frequent relays of active men. Transference over the churchyard wall was easy in a dark evening; and once in the street, the carrier of the sack drew no attention at so early an hour.'

Note that the shroud was 'scrupulously buried again' after the snatch. In England, theft of a naked body was less heinous than the theft of grave-clothes which was a serious crime south of the border. However, in Scotland, there was no distinction between the two offences, which were, and are, dealt with under the charge of 'violating the sepulchres of the dead.' To avoid possible identification and court action, the culprits left the shroud behind.

But bodysnatchers could avoid back-breaking toil by offering bribes to sextons or relatives of the deceased.

In 1825 the *Kelso Mail* reported: 'Those who follow the infamous employment of stealing bodies are now contriving, instead of taking them out of graves, to steal them before they are buried.'

Sextons were bribed to provide weak fastenings on coffins. But one grave-digger hit on a novel method. After mourners had departed he would open the coffin and remove the body, placing it in a sack. He would fill the grave with earth, at each stage lifting the body near the surface. Finally, the 'subject' lay hidden under a light blanket of soil, ready to be uplifted that during the hours of darkness.

At Glenbervie, in the Kincardineshire Mearns, nifty detective work by the minister, Rev. James Drummond, averted an injustice after a grave was robbed. The finger of suspicion pointed at John Clark, faithful grave-digger and beadle. The kirk elders threatened to resign if Clark went unpunished. But the minister pointed out that Clark, when digging a fresh grave, always piled the earth on a particular side. The bodysnatchers had been less precise and dumped the soil on the opposite side. A scandal was averted.

Bodies were transported to the anatomists by land and sea. They were delivered by porters to medical colleges and extra-mural schools after a journey by stagecoach or horse-drawn cart.

A pamphlet written by *The Echo of Surgeons Square* (the author was probably the embittered Davie Paterson, sacked by Dr Knox after the trial of Burke) lifted the lid on the methods of transporting bodies by the Edinburgh coach from Newcastle. Trunks or hampers either bore a false address or no address, but an advice note would be forwarded to the coach office giving details of the delivery. Items would be marked soft goods, crystal or stationery. An agent claimed the package, paid the carriage and ensured its safe deposit in Surgeons' Square. Because of the mix-up at the coach company's offices in Edinburgh, 'Echo' alleged a box delivered to a lecture in February 1829 contained, instead of a corpse, a ham, a cheese, eggs and a bundle of Hodden grey cloth. It was presumed that the dead body had been sent to an innocent party!

One day 'Echo' rounded the corner of the square to see two men, bearing a coffin on their shoulders, run at the trot into a lecture room with the body of a female. The corpse, which had been partly dissected, was stolen from the Royal Infirmary, a rich source for resurrectionists claiming to be the kin of persons dying without friends or relatives.

In Sanquhar, near Dumfries, at the time of the bodysnatching panic, weavers were standing in groups on the street enjoying a smoke, when a gig with a lady and gentleman drove into the town from the west, and pulled up at the inn at the Townfoot, tenanted by Andrew Lamont.

The driver handed the reins to a boy, then entered the inn where he ordered a glass of whisky, which he drank standing up. The stranger was asked if he had travelled far and was he going to treat his good wife to a dram. The man said he had come from Ayrshire and that his wife never took spirits. The lady, heavily veiled, and with a plaid drawn round her, sat erect in the trap. There was a certain stiffness about her posture and when the horse moved forward it was noticed a rope was passed round her body and fastened to the seat.

William Wilson (1830-1908), writing in 1902, said: 'A shout immediately got up that it was a corpse the man had beside him, and a rush was made for the gig. But, putting the whip to the horse, the stranger quickly got away, and the steed dashed down the street at full gallop.'

The weavers gave chase, and one bold man made a grab for the resurrectionist, but the driver lashed out, and the gig sped into the Dumfries-shire countryside. 'Who he was, where he had come from, and whither he was going with his ghastly companion was never found out.'

Scotland, at the time of the resurrectionists, was swept by similar tales, invented or otherwise. In Aberdeen it was said a doctor had entered the College-gate in a gig with a lady beside him. In Aberdeen, William Buchanan wrote: 'It was no other than a corpse dressed up as a ruse to deceive the public. Someone who saw the gig declared that the lady was a corpse. It went round the town like lightning and a great concourse of people assembled round the College-gate and threatened a breach of the peace.'

One vehicle marked down by the general public for use by the bodysnatchers was the Noddy, a nippy, two-wheeled horse-drawn cab, so called because of the jerking action of passengers as it sped over cobbled streets. In North-east Scotland, medical students were nicknamed 'Noddies' by travelling folk, probably because of their mode of transport in country regions. The doctors were branded 'burkers'.

Stolen bodies were smuggled across the Forth in ferry-boats plying twice-a-day between Leith, the port of Edinburgh, and Fife.

Innocently marked tea-boxes made the one-hour trip from Pettycur, if the weather was favourable. The resurrectionists would usually dispatch the empty containers by an earlier boat from Edinburgh and they would be collected by an accomplice, and held in safe-keeping. The ferries were known as 'Kinghorn boats' long after they had stopped sailing from the Fife port.

In December 1818, three professional resurrectionists, led by John Wilson, hired a carter to take the bodies of Elizabeth Neish, a weaver's widow, and drowned seaman Richard Lockhart, lifted at Dysart, to Pettycur. Wilson told his cronies to tell the carter they were smuggling whisky.

But the stench from a box gave the game away and, when

45

the ferry docked at Leith, Wilson was arrested when he went to collect his goods. Yet in January 1819, Wilson was the only culprit to stand at the bar in the High Court in Edinburgh. He was locked up for nine months.

Chapter 5
Bells, Bodies and Booby-Traps

The ghoulish activities of the snatchers led to the Scottish public adopting a wide range of methods for safeguarding the dead.

The purpose of the mort-safe was to encage the coffin until the corpse was beyond dissection.

A simple method of protection proved effective – at first. A heavy slab of stone placed on top of a fresh coffin defied the efforts of raiding parties. It was just too heavy for them to move. In 1816, Superintendent Gibb of Aberdeen Harbour Works allayed the fears of Torry fisherfolk by gifting a huge, dressed mort-stone to St Fittick's Kirkyard. It cost 2s 6d (12.5 pence) to transport the stone by cart from the ferry landing stage to the kirkyard.

When grave-diggers at Kemnay, Aberdeenshire, lifted a mort-stone for another funeral they were puzzled at first to find leaves in the grave. It was recollected, however, that on the night after the burial there had been a violent gale. They concluded the leaves had blown into the open grave when an attempt was made to lift the stone by resurrectionists.

But the bodysnatchers soon found a method of getting out the corpse without removing the stone and a new design was introduced.

The iron mort-safe – a substantial cage or shell – was peculiar to Scotland. In 1819, an English writer noted: 'The iron cage or safe is a Scotch invention which we have lately seen at Glasgow.' Relatives were charged a shilling a day for its use. The 'Aberdeenshire mort-safe' comprised of a coffin-shaped stone with a 'skirt' of iron lattice-work.

Four fine examples of this type of safe sit in front of Miss Elyza Fraser's Mausoleum at Cluny.

The mort-safe used by Quakers at Kinmuck, near Inverurie, was said to have been designed by Peter Brownie, the former snatcher who worked with 'Resurrectionist' Marr of Newhills.

The safe is entirely comprised of lattice-work halves which resembled a clam when bolted together with the coffin inside. The safe was so heavy when loaded that it needed ten men to lower it into the grave, and to lift it again. An iron nut-key was used for turning the bolts which fastened the mort-safe together. The mort-safe has been preserved in an Aberdeen museum.

In North-east Scotland, iron mort-safes were nicknamed 'irons'. At Inverurie, Aberdeenshire, heavy block and tackle, suspended on sheer poles, was used to lower and lift the shell. The tackle was stored in Mr Gray's bakery for safekeeping. It was a good choice for it meant it was watched night and day. It is now in the care of Aberdeenshire Heritage.

The Don Valley was a happy hunting ground for Aberdeen medical students, which accounts for the area being rich in surviving mort-safes. In 1906, an unusually designed mort-safe was unearthed with great difficulty at Tough. It consisted of a cage bolted into a heavy stone at each end. The cage was empty but because the mort-safe was intact, it was decided the contents had decayed and crumbled into dust. An old lady recalled how the deceased had lived in fear of the bodysnatchers. A relative of the dead man was enclosed in a similar mort-safe and now rests in peace in the churchyard at Alford. Both men were related to a local doctor, who no doubt warned them of the tricks of the trade.

Fear of falling into the clutches of an anatomist lingered after the days of bodysnatching.

At Banchory-Devenick a local builder donated an iron, coffin-shaped mort-safe, which sits in a corner of the graveyard, but a simpler design was used more than 30 years after the scourge of the snatchers. In 1854, two huge mort-stones protected the coffin of a young man whose father feared his body would fall into the hands of the doctors. The stones came to light in 1911.

The design of mort-safes varied throughout the country, but the coffin-shaped box remained popular. The 1828 example from Airth, near Stirling, exhibited at the Museum of Scotland in Edinburgh, has a detachable lid in two halves. There is also a corpse collar, or mort collar, from Kingskettle, Fife. It was bolted through the bottom of the coffin and round the neck of the corpse to prevent theft.

In the river-bank kirkyard at Logierait in Perthshire a rough-stoned enclosure contains three unusual iron-grilled safes, one child's size.

Mort-safes were the work of the local smiddy. The blacksmith at Dalkeith supplied mort-safes for Earlston in Berwickshire.

Amid the gothic grandeur of Greyfriars Churchyard in Edinburgh's old town, are several examples of mort-safes. Many mouldering graveyards in the city resemble zoological gardens.

The 17th-century lychgate at the Auld Kirk of Ayr is adorned with relics. Historic St Mary's Tower in Dundee also has a mort-safe.

A huge iron mort-safe at Colinton, where his grandfather was minister and now lies buried, would have fired the youthful imagination of Robert Louis Stevenson. That, and the tales of grave-robbers passed to him by his nurse, 'Cummy'. Indeed, Alison Cunnigham's mother, dying in 1870, ordered she not be buried among her relatives in Torryburn kirkyard on the north bank of the Firth of Forth, but in the town cemetery, where the bodysnatchers would be unable to molest her.

Unfortunately, mort-safes were not a sufficient deterrent. It became the custom for organised groups of armed vigilantes to keep watch on fresh graves. Temporary shelters, such as canvas tents, eventually led to more solid and comfortable accommodation. Soon, squat, stone-built watch-houses and watch-towers appeared in churchyards from the Borders to the Highlands. A historian noted that the kirkyards of Daviot and Dunlichity 'are enclosed with substantial stone walls, and a night watch-house has been erected in each.' The 1820 watch-house at Dunlichity in Strathnairn is a sturdy, two-storeyed structure.

The watch-house at Oldhamstocks, near Dunbar, is inscribed: 'It shall not be plucked up nor thrown down anymore forever. Jeremiah. 31,40. Erected by Mrs Agnes Moore, 1824'. (She was the minister's wife).

Watch-houses are sometimes confused with offertory and session houses found at the gateway of old kirks.

A Speyside historian, James Thomson, gave a vivid description of the watch-house at Aberlour on Speyside.

It was built of rough stones about ten feet square and stood on a spot overlooking the whole of the graveyard.

'On either side of the door was a narrow slit or window that opened and closed with strong wooden shutters,' wrote Thomson in the *Moray and Nairn Express* in August 1885. 'Through these apertures the watchers could reconnoitre unobserved, and, if need be fire their guns upon the desecrators of the grave.'

Thomson went on: 'The fire place was opposite the door, and over it hung two claymores that had done service at Culloden; upon a small table in the centre of the apartment lay an open Bible, a snuffmull, pipes, and a bottle of uisgebeatha stood there to refresh the weary watchers. Had the staunchest teetotaller been there, he would have been sorely tempted to fill the quaich and taste the contents of the bottle.' Thomson referred to the hardships faced by the male population of the small parish during the six weeks required to watch over a recent interment. The watch-house in some cases was occupied throughout the winter months when an epidemic swept the neighbourhood.

Aberlour was the scene of a hilarious episode involving the death of a suspected witch and two members of the watch. The menfolk were reluctant to keep guard on the woman's grave because of her reputation of being in league with the devil. But when a much-respected parishioner died at the same time Jamie Gordon and Johnny Dustan agreed to 'watch the dead'.

During the watch the pair got ready to patrol the graves. Lantern in hand, Jamie undid the bolt, lifted the latch, and was about to step out into the November darkness when something charged. The table was upset and the lamp and lantern extinguished. By the glow from the fireplace they realised they were dealing with a fearful beast.

Yelled Johnny: 'Save yerself, Jamie. We're in the power o' the enemy. God gie us a gweed riddance.'

Fearing the dead witch had conjured up an evil spirit, the pair fled the scene. Next morning they returned to the graveyard with townsfolk to try and solve the mystery.

It was a local character, Jock Fleming, who corralled the culprit. He hooted with laughter and jibed: 'Ye are a' fools the gither. Tibbies quiet enough in her lair. Here's the beast that beat ye baith.' Glowering from under a nearby tablestone was Duncan Macpherson's ram.

The evil-tempered ram lived with its Highland master and his nine children, sharing their humble home and meals. But it was the terror of the parish when on the loose.

Whisky was freely available to the night watch at Aberlour, it seems, but imbibing was frowned upon by kirk sessions. Orders of watch at Carmunnock in Lanarkshire in 1828 banned alcohol. Watchmen were warned about deserting their posts during the night. Two men had to mount guard at sunset and remain on duty until darkness lifted in winter, or at sunrise in the summer months. They were forbidden to have visitors, unless they knew the password for that particular night. They had to remain silent, unless giving the alarm. Damage to furniture and fittings in the watch-house meant a fine. But, as we have seen, rules were made to be broken.

The session at Kirkliston, West Lothian, allowed the watch a drop of whisky to keep them warm in December 1818. Two years later the watchers smashed the kirk windows, but whether booze was the cause is not known.

In one North-east parish a decayed burial vault was converted into a watch-house. A rotten floor lay between the watchmen and the tombs below. Discipline was slack he watch and visitors would pass the time drinking gambling.

One eventful night a larger gathering than usual crowded into the watch-house. It was later said they spent the evening 'in a pastime very much out of place amongst the dead.' The jollity was cut short when the floor gave way and the riotous company ended up in the vault. In clearing out the debris next morning a pack of cards was found 'with more broken glass than goes to the making of one bottle.' At Old Marnoch, Banffshire, they built a small schoolroom over the vault!

Tales of the Scottish bodysnatchers are filled with such incidents following a night of revelry. At the cliff-top chapel of St Mary-of-the-Storms at Cowie, overlooking Stonehaven Bay, a group of watchmen became itchy-fingered when a colleague spotted 'something black', which appeared to move then stand still. Excitement and alcohol got the better of them and they opened fire. The black object vanished with a thud. 'Weel, lads,' growled the oldest member of the group, 'we maun see what damage we've deen; he's maybe only wounded.' On investigation they found they had shot a tombstone which had toppled and broken. On their way back to Cowie village they met a party of confused coastguards who had seen the flash of gunfire and believed it was a distress signal from a shipwreck.

A holed gravestone in the kirkyard at Kilmonivaig, near Spean Bridge, is the result of a shot fired by the sexton when he suspected bodysnatchers were ready to pounce.

At Fala, Midlothian, watchers shot the minister's goat by mistake.

Trigger-happy watchers proved a problem for officials in Old Aberdeen in late winter of 1809. The burgh records state: 'Complaints having been made of people using fire arms in the churchyard at night, when watching the bodies of their deceased friends, whereby danger and inconvenience may arise.'

It was recommended public notices prohibiting the nuisance be posted, and the clergy asked to issue warnings from the pulpit.

Mansie Wauch, the fictional tailor of Dalkeith, had an imaginary brush with 'The Resurrection Men' after the local kirkyard was raided. Mansie's nerves were jangling before he set foot in the graveyard. He had been paired with a teenage boy to keep watch in the session-house one dark and stormy November night. Armed with a flintlock borrowed from his neighbour Mansie was more a danger to himself than any 'unearthly resurrection men', wrapped up in dreadnought coats, with blackened faces and wielding pistols and cudgels.

Night noises in the darkened graveyard beyond the door of the session-house frightened the pair. Isaac, a local worthy, gained entry after giving the password, 'Copmahagen', then proceeded to heighten their terror with tales of spooks, witches, Irish medical students and grave-robbers.

The cantrips ended abruptly when a bottle of brown stout, placed too close to the roaring fire, cast its cork with a loud bang. Mansie fainted.

Christison, later Sir Robert, a future Victorian president of the British Medical Association, who probably took part in the raid described below, accused the watch in one rural area of cowardice.

The place chosen for the raid by medical students was a lonely churchyard seven miles from Edinburgh, separated from the highway by a hedge, a hollow grass field and the kirkyard wall.

He wrote in his memoirs: 'On arriving at the place, they observed light issuing from the vestry window. A scout was therefore sent across the field to reconnoitre. His companions, by the light of a young moon, could see him crawl over the wall, when the vestry door opened, a man stepped out in bright light, a shot went off, the scout dropped down motionless at the foot of the wall, and the shooter retired within the vestry and shut the door.'

A second scout was sent to check when the first student appeared, and laughingly explained he had merely ducked when the watchman fired. They remained quiet for half-an-hour, when the 'farce of firing was repeated, to frighten away depredators, and satisfy the parish that watch was faithfully kept. Taking advantage of the discovery that the churchyard was never patrolled, the spoilers entered it during an interval between the alarms; and as their object lay on the other side of the church from the vestry, they carried on their operation, with a short interruption as firing-time came round, completed their work, and decamped with their plunder.'

Watch-houses, as we have seen, were simple gabled structures, though one Berwickshire shelter is prefabricated from ancient tombstones bearing carved symbols of mortality.

The watch-house at Edinkillie Kirk, Dunphail in Moray, is hexagonal and topped with a ball-finial, while the quaint-looking watch-house at Mortlach Parish Church, Dufftown, has gothic-arched windows.

At the end of the second decade of the 19th century watch-towers were sometimes preferred to watch-houses. At Banchory-Ternan on Royal Deeside the two-storey tower was built in 1829.

It comes complete with conical roof, chimney and bellcote for the bell, cast by a Dutch bellfounder in 1664. It originally hung in St Ternan's parish church, demolished in 1775. The bell was tolled to warn parishioners of grave-robbers. Windows ensured a close watch on all corners of the graveyard.

The tower has a gun port which doubled as the aperture for the bell rope. The custom was to fire the gun intermittently to ward off intruders. The East Parish Church Men's Group spearheaded the project, and the restoration work was carried out by mason Alistair Urquhart in 1998.

St Cuthbert's in Edinburgh, has a circular watch-tower, dated 1827, close by the steps at Lothian Road. It was restored in 1990, with added flag pole. There's a dinky replica at Eckford in Roxburghshire. But the capital's New Calton burial ground in Regent Road boasts a three-storey tower with crenellated parapet. Its windows, now blocked, covered every inch of the graveyard, as well as offering guards a panoramic view of the old town and beyond.

Duddingston has a crenellated hexagon, two storeys high, the lower used as a vestry and session house.

A two-storey rectangular watch-tower, formerly with a forestair, at Lumphanan, is now private property.

At first the people mounting guard from sunset to sunrise were relatives and friends of the deceased. But in time communal watching societies were formed. The North Quarter Friendly Churchyard Guard Association was established in 1823 to protect Glasgow's High Churchyard. It could call on two thousand members. Night patrols avoided using firearms and cutlasses, preferring cudgels instead. Watching societies funded themselves. The Paisley Society for Protecting the Dead, formed in January 1829, relied on subscription fees from a membership totalling seven thousand by the end of its first year. They undertook to share the duty of watching every night. Wooden boxes, each with a grate for a fire, were provided and the result was highly successful.

When the Bridgeton Grave Protection Society was formed in Glasgow in 1824 a song helped raise spirits at a fund-raising event. It was entitled 'Ye who mourn your dear departed.'

At least two Scots left instructions in their wills in the hope of a blessed resurrection. Wealthy Edinburgh citizen, Louis Cauvin, directed in 1823 that: 'My corpse is to be deposited in Restalrig and watched for a proper time. The door of the tomb must be taken off, and the space built up strongly with ashlar stones. The tomb must be shut forever, and never opened.'

At Kilrenny, Fife, eccentric John Ramsay wished to be buried close to his mother on the 'sunny side of Kilrenny Kirk, under a big red stone, ten feet deep, to keep my body from the inhuman monsters – the Resurrection men.'

It later became the fashion to replace the cumbersome mort-safes of stone and iron with the mort-house. The idea was to give night watchers some respite.

The public vault, which was usually funded by public subscription, was a rectangular stone cell, partly or wholly subterranean, and entered by a stout iron door. The 1826 battlemented dead house at Crail in Fife bears the inscription: 'Erected for securing the dead.'

At Fintray, Aberdeenshire, the inner walls of the vault, built in 1830, were lined with sheet metal for protection against mildew. Coffins lay on iron shelves, while the iron door would prevent unlawful entry. But it was not impregnable. Soon after its inauguration a local farmer was snatched and his headless corpse found dumped in a sack on a nearby road.

The Culsalmond vault, which is being restored, provided a source of income for the parish kirk. The walls were thick and the iron door doubly fashioned with keys placed in custody of four keepers, who were elected periodically. The mortuary attracted custom from as far as Banff, Portsoy and Cullen.

Non-subscribers were charged 10 shillings (50p) to five shillings (25p), depending on status, while locals paid as little as 3d. A leaking coffin meant a repair job by a carpenter and a £1 fine for the deceased's family.

St Columba's at Belhelvie, up the coast from Aberdeen, has two mort-houses. One is a turfed and vaulted chamber with no date. The second (1835) has an oak door with bar over keyholes for extra security. Two coffin shelves are fitted with rollers.

This vault was used in later years to house bodies of drowned fishermen washed up on the nearby beach. Rules drawn up for its maintenance and care are extant.

A unique circular mort-house was completed at Udny Green in Aberdeenshire in the year the Anatomy Act rendered it obsolete. The 'Round House' has two doors – an outer one of sturdy oak and studded with iron bolts – and an inner iron door.

There were four key-holders, including the parish minister, Rev. John Leslie.

Coffins were placed on an oak carousel which revolved

to make space for newcomers.

When the coffin had completed the full circuit and reappeared in the inner doorway it was ready for burial. The vault cost £114 to build, although £5 was deducted from the mason's account because it was thought he had not conformed to the contract.

The vault and its maintenance costs were paid by subscription. No corpse was allowed to remain in the vault for longer than three months, and a committee ensured the strict regulations were obeyed.

At the height of the bodysnatching terror extreme methods were introduced to protect the dead. The grave was booby-trapped. The most obvious method was the use of the spring-gun or man-trap. An oft-repeated tale concerned three medical students who slipped into Blackfriars churchyard in Glasgow to steal a body. One student stumbled over a trip-wire and was killed instantly.

His companions, fearing a scandal if they abandoned their friend's body, adopted a macabre method of carrying away his body. They propped the body up between them, then tied the corpse's legs to theirs, at the ankles, placed his arms over their shoulders, and staggered through the darkened streets singing loudly. At their lodgings they laid the deceased in his bed and put it out that he had committed suicide.

In 1810, a Dundee father devised a highly-dangerous method of protecting his daughter's body from bodysnatchers who might slip past the watch at the 'Auld Howff' cemetery.

It was recorded the distraught parent had attached a small box 'enclosing some deathful apparatus' to the top of his daughter's coffin. Before the coffin was lowered into the grave a large quantity of gunpowder was poured into the box and the 'landmine' primed. Anyone who attempted to lift the body would risk being maimed or killed. The sexton feared an instant explosion and stood back in alarm after throwing the shovelful of earth into the grave, as was the custom.

The Dundee case was not the only example of a booby-trapped coffin. Scots bodysnatchers were known to cross the border into Northern England to mount raids on lonely churchyards.

In February 1824, *The Carlisle Journal* reported:

'Some bodies having been stolen from the churchyard of a remote parish in Northumberland, the owner of the estate, to prevent such depradation in future, has directed the graves to be made rather shorter than the coffin, and to be excavated at the bottom so as to admit the head under the solid ground. It is then impossible to raise it by the feet and the ground must be cut away above the head – a work of more time than could always be commanded by the operation.

'In addition, a mixture of percussion powder and gunpowder, placed on a wire in the inside of the coffin, to explode on its being opened, has been resorted to. This will retain its explosive power for a month, in which time the corpse will be generally unfit for dissection.'

Grim Warning: The Latin inscription on the gates of St Peter's Cemetery, Aberdeen, means 'Not for self but for all'.

Watch-house at St Fittick's Kirkyard at the Bay of Nigg, Aberdeen, where the theft of the body of Mrs Spark outraged the community.

For whom the bell tolls? The watch-tower at Banchory-Ternan, on Royal Deeside, after restoration in 1998.

Guardians of the dead: the watch-house and mort-safe at Banchory-Devenick, Aberdeenshire. (Photo: N.G. Adams)

'Round House', Udny Green, Aberdeenshire. The vault was a Home Guard armoury in World War 2. (Photo: N. G. Adams)

Tower of strength: the three-storey watch-tower at the New Calton graveyard, Edinburgh, offered panoramic views.

61

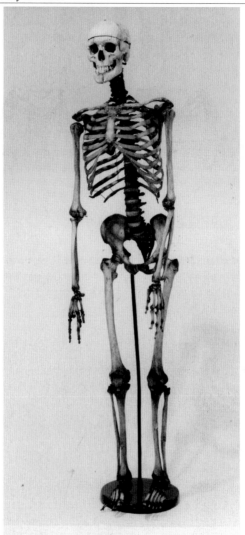

The skeleton of William Burke is preserved in the anatomy museum at Edinburgh University. (Photo courtesy: Division of Bio-Medical and Clinical Laboratory Sciences, Edinburgh University)

Burke and Hare never robbed a grave. They murdered for profit, but only William Burke was hanged. These sketches were made during their trial. (From John Macnee's Trial of William Burke and Helen McDougal)

Gothic horror: spectators flee Dr Ure's galvanic experiment on the murderer Matthew Clydesdale in Glasgow, 1818. (from an old French print)

The 1827 watch-tower at St Cuthbert's, Edinburgh, where burials were first recorded in the 16th century.

The design of the iron mort-safe, a Scottish invention, varied. This example can be seen at Greyfriars Kirkyard, Edinburgh.

Three iron-grilled mort-safes, one child's size, at Logierait, Perthshire.

Border guard: the watch-tower at Eckford, Roxburghshire. (Photo: Ninian Reid)

Mort-safes were the work of local blacksmiths. The Airth mort-safe, made in 1828, is exhibited at the Museum of Scotland.

During World War Two scrap iron was collected, but this inverted mort-safe at Tough, Donside, survived.

The turf-roofed dead house at Coull, Royal Deeside. Snatchers fled empty handed after a notable raid.

Greyfriars Kirkyard: many old Edinburgh graveyards resemble zoos with barred tombs to deter bodysnatchers.

Dance of death: the jigging skeleton of Greyfriars Kirkyard, complete with surgical instruments, is a grotesque memorial to the surgeon, John Borthwick of Stow.

Surgeons' Square, Edinburgh, 1829. Burke and Hare delivered their victims to Dr Knox's lecture rooms (centre). (From Cassell's Old and New Edinburgh*).*

Chapter 6
Not Wanted on Voyage

In 1825, the rapid growth of steam navigation in Dublin, combined with the high price of bodies being touted around anatomists in Edinburgh and elsewhere, led to an illegal export trade in corpses from impoverished Ireland.

Paddle steamers sailed for Scottish ports with holds containing boxes purporting to be limestone or even cheese or pickled herrings. It was vital they reached their destination before the real contents turned ripe.

Glasgow chronicler, Peter Mackenzie, claimed in his colourful memoirs that an Irish sloop arrived at the Broomielaw with a consignment of cotton or linen rags, addressed to a huxter in the city's Jamaica Street. He refused to accept the cargo because the freight charges amounted to an improbable sum of between £50 and £60, payable on delivery. The carriers transported the bales to a quayside warehouse, where, after a few days, an awful stench arose. Customs officers inspected the cargo and found the cause was the putrefied bodies of men, women and children. The rag merchant had not received word of the macabre cargo from his contact in Dublin. The Glasgow magistrates ordered the dead bodies to be buried in the graveyard at Anderston.

The chief gang of Irish resurrectionists was led by a Scotsman, William or Wilson Rae, an army surgeon on half pay, who lived in the Dublin area of Sandymount, convenient to the cross channel steamers.

Dublin-based Dr John Fleetwood, senior, who has written, broadcasted and lectured on the history of the Irish 'stiffy-lifters', has suggested that Rae might have been the Aberdeen medical student who fled the country after his involvement in the farcical theft of Mrs Spark's body at St Fittick's, Old Torry (see chapter 2).

Rae was highly organised. He stored bodies at home before shipment. One of the members of his gang was a compliant captain of a steam packet. His crew were also in on the secret. Some crooked police and customs officers were in his pay.

On the mainland the price of a body reached astronomical proportions, compared to Dublin prices. In Dublin a stolen body could sometimes fetch a few shillings, but the maximum recorded price for Irish bodies on the London market was £38 for an assortment of three in December 1831.

One of Rae's severest critics was Peter Hennis Greene, who contributed to the *Lancet*. Greene, who had taken part in bodysnatching, and wrote under the pseudonym of Erinensis, described the resurrectionist, among other things, as a 'carcase merchant', 'despicable mercenary Scotsman' and 'the wholesale vampire.'

The writer compared some surgeons unfavourably with the resurrectionists declaring the latter had 'done as much for our fame as all the surgeons put together'. He was opposed to the export trade, fearing Irish medical schools would suffer.

He called for Dublin teachers to unite to control the bodysnatching business, and even warned that a heavy demand on the Irish market could tempt local resurrectionists to emulate Burke and Hare.

The activities of Rae and his associates outraged the general public. The Irish bodysnatchers left a trail of desecration after each raid. Smashed tomb ornaments, holes in the ground, and naked corpses abandoned on the dockside. Two other notorious exporters were Collins and Daly, who eventually held Dublin anatomy schools to ransom by increasing the price of a 'thing' for the surgeon by 800%!

Stolen bodies, whether for the domestic or export market, were sometimes stored at the College of Surgeons in Dublin. In January 1828 a rumour swept the city that a body due for export was on the premises. In the subsequent riot a college porter, Luke Redmond, was killed. Another College porter, Christopher Dixon, was repeatedly dunked in the

Liffey until he was half-drowned.

But it was the reckless method of shipping cadavers across the Irish Sea that infuriated the Irish public. The *Cork Advertiser* reported a failed attempt to ship bodies by the Erin Steam packet from Eden Quay in Dublin. A customer had handed over a large cask to the shipping agents claiming it contained 'pickled gullets'. But during the day the office clerks reported a 'most noisome and offensive smell' emitting from the cask. That evening it was shipped to the vessel which was moored in the river opposite the Customs House.

The *Advertiser* report continued: 'It had not remained there long however when some of those on board happened to step on its lid which immediately gave way under the weight, fell in and discovered to view the appalling contents – two human bodies, one that of a female, the other of a male, having the backs and limbs doubled up and squeezed together so as to make them fit within the narrow limits of the vessel in which they were stowed, the only substance between them and it being some straw thinly strewed beneath the lid.

'The circumstance having come to the notice of the police, two constables were dispatched from Henry Street Police Office to take charge during the night of the bodies which still remained in the open cask close by the side of the vessel. We have not heard that the miscreant concerned in this inhuman traffic in the dead has yet been traced and who certainly deserves to be punished to the utmost rigour that the law permits in such cases; as independent of the offence constituted by the stealing of the bodies from their receptacles the crime must be considerably aggravated by the danger to which the health of the living passengers in the vessel must have been exposed from inhaling the noxious effluvia emitted by the carcasses remaining during the voyage in such close contact with them had not chance fortunately detected the attempted imposition.'

In 1828, corpses bound for Glasgow and other British ports were stored in a depot at the rear of Bachelor's Walk, near Eden Quay, on the banks of the Liffey. They were deposited there until a sufficient number constituted a cargo.

When police swooped on a vessel about to leave Belfast for Glasgow in July 1823 they uncovered a corpse-smuggling operation between the two cities. They were following up a lead about a certain barrel that had been put on board by a porter. The barrel was found to contain the bodies of a middle-aged female and a young child packed in sawdust. The trail led to a house in Academy Street, Belfast, where two men named Stewart and Feeney had stored picks, shovels and barrels in readiness for their next expedition. The pair was traced to their lodgings in Cadell's Entry. Stewart managed to give the law the slip but his partner in crime was blind drunk and arrested.

A search of the premises revealed a box addressed to Stewart with a label indicating it had originated in Edinburgh. At the bottom of the box they found a brass syringe used to inject the veins of dead bodies, a surgeon's knife, forceps and five sovereigns. The fate of Stewart and Feeney is unknown.

The earliest known Irish reference to the illegal supply of dead bodies for dissection appeared in Faulkner's *Dublin Journal* in May 1732. A grave-digger in St Andrew's churchyard was jailed for co-operating with bodysnatchers. His successor, Richard Fox, escaped from custody while facing a similar charge.

St Andrew's was a popular hunting ground for the Dublin resurrectionists. In 1825, George Hendrick, who went by the bizarre sobriquet, 'Crazy Crow', was fined and jailed for snatching there. The eccentric Hendrick handed out his picture with the following poem, probably written by himself:

'With look ferocious and with beer replete
See Crazy Crow beneath his minstrel weight
His voice as frightful as great Etna's roar
Which spreads its horrors to the distant shore.
Equally hideous is his well-known face
Murders each ear till whiskey makes it cease.'

The poetic Crazy Crow became a porter for Dublin musicians, hence the reference to his 'minstrel weight.' He died in 1862.

In the annals of 18th- and early 19th-century Dublin medical history, bodysnatching was first carried out by amateurs – eager, young medical students and their helpers. But that changed as the porters and pupils were driven from the graveyards by large numbers of desperate men, the scum of Dublin's underworld. The schools became dependant for the supply of corpses upon those professional criminals, whatever the price.

The ironically-named Prospect Cemetery, better known as Glasnevin, on the north side of Dublin, was a regular target of the bodysnatchers. It was ringed with seven watch-towers, and bloodhounds roamed its dark acres at night.

In January 1830 a fierce pitched battle disrupted the peace of the old burial ground when a gang of grimly-determined resurrectionists attempted to steal the body of Edward Barrett, Esq. The watchers, made up of members of the local gentry, spotted three or four snatchers standing on the cemetery wall, with several others attempting to join them.

The account in Saunder's *News Letter*, which regularly published the activities of the snatchers, reads like an episode from the Wild West:

'The party in the churchyard warned them off, and were replied to by a discharge from firearms. This brought on a general engagement; the Sack-'Em-Up gentlemen fired from behind the churchyard wall, by which they were defended while their opponents on the watch fired from behind the tombstones. Upwards of 58 to 60 shots were fired, one of the body snatchers was seen to fall; his body was carried off by his companions. Some of them are supposed to have been severely wounded, as a great quantity of blood was observed outside the churchyard wall, notwithstanding the ground was covered with snow. During the firing, which continued for upwards of a quarter of an hour, the church bell was rung by one of the watchmen, which, with the discharge from the firearms, collected several of the townspeople and the police to the spot – several of the former, not withstanding the severity of the weather, in nearly a state of nakedness; but the assailants were by this time defeated and effected their retreat. Several headstones bear evident marks of the conflict, being struck with balls etc.'

Shortly afterwards armed guards opened up on bodysnatchers as they clambered over the wall at Glasnevin. Some of the gang members were wounded as they fled, for blood was found on the wall.

The old stable yard, where the Glasnevin bloodhounds were kept, is still known as the 'dog yard'. One of the former watch-towers now acts as a chimney of the present crematorium! In post-resurrectionist times, the dogs remained in residence. On one occasion they attacked a doctor called to treat one of the staff. They probably associated his medical odour with the bodysnatchers they had been trained to attack.

'Bully's Acre' at the Royal Military Hospital at Kilmainham, had provided rich pickings for Dublin snatchers since the 18th century. In 1760, medical students stole the body of the Irish giant, Cornelius Magrath, after posing as mourners at his funeral. They plied his relatives with whiskey laced with opium then bore off the body in triumph. The drunken relatives buried a coffin filled with stones.

Belfast, like Dublin and most Irish cities, had watch-houses and watch-towers, and other devices to baulk the bodysnatchers. As well as local 'stiffy-lifters', the Belfast public were troubled by resurrectionists from across the water. In 1823 a gang of Scots were thrown into the lock-up at Carrickfergus after mounting a raid on the local burial yard.

The authorities in Scotland and Ireland were outraged at the sickening export trade, although one Edinburgh newspaper took an extreme view. It criticised official interference with the shipment of Irish bodies arguing that 'for every Irish subject they seize they insure the rifling of some Scottish grave.'

Dead bodies also made the shorter sea passage to Liverpool, where they were sorted out before being forwarded to anatomists throughout the mainland. But horror was in the air.

In October 1826 three casks marked, 'Bitter Salts', were loaded on board the smack, *Latona*, bound for Glasgow and addressed to 'Mr G.H. Ironson', of Edinburgh. The dockers complained about the stench from the casks to the customs officers.

The casks had been stored in the cellar of a respectable boarding school for young gentlemen in Hope Street, Liverpool. Investigators found the bodies of twenty-two adults and babies. At the subsequent trial of three Scotsmen details of the grisly find sickened the foreman of the jury. The ring-leader, James Donaldson, was sent to the Kirkdale House of Correction for 12 months, and fined £50. His accomplices, John Ross and Patrick McGregor each received 12 months and a £25 fine.

By 1828, the Edinburgh anatomist Robert Knox had become a leading importer of Irish bodies. In the winter session of 1828-9 he had 504 students on his books, and he paid hundreds of pounds out of his own pocket to ensure there would not be a shortage of fresh bodies.

The irascible Knox, however, was forced to pen a letter to Home Secretary Robert Peel when Dublin anatomists took a tough line over the wholesale export of Irish bodies. He accused them of obstructiveness.

He complained: 'During the course of last summer, two cases containing anatomical subjects were shipped on board a steam packet in Dublin Harbour. A few hours previous to the sailing of the vessel, one of the lecturers in Dublin, who had probably received information of the shipment, sent his assistant on board, who, suspecting the boxes to contain subjects, procured a warrant, had them broken up and their contents left exposed on the quay, for, as I am informed, the space of two days, apparently for the purpose of irritating the populace and preventing the supply of the schools; and this at a time when subjects abounded so much in Dublin that to use a mercantile phrase, the article was in no demand whatever.'

Knox usually sent an assistant to Dublin to select suitable 'subjects'. He also complained to Peel that anatomical material sent to him, via Liverpool, got no further than the Mersey port's Brunswick Dock where it was opened and impounded. At Carlisle the previous winter the authorities broke open, on mere suspicion, a package being carried north on the Edinburgh coach. Some days before writing the memorandum packages containing Edinburgh-bound specimens were seized at Greenock. Knox never posted the letter. That weekend Burke and Hare were arrested.

Chapter 7
The Fiends

> Up the close and doon the stair,
> But and ben wi' Burke and Hare.
> Burke's the butcher, Hare's the thief,
> Knox the boy that buys the beef.
> (Popular ballad)

In the dead of winter 1827, two Irishmen bundled a dead body into a sack and delivered it to Dr Robert Knox's establishment at No 10 Surgeons' Square in Edinburgh. They had been redirected to the address after they had accosted a young man in the quadrangle of the College, and made inquiries about another anatomist, Dr Monro. By a sheer stroke of fate, they had run across one of Dr Knox's pupils, who promptly recommended they deal with Knox instead.

They duly handed over the body to three of Knox's assistants, William Fergusson, Thomas Wharton Jones and Alexander Miller, who, in time, would become eminent surgeons. They were paid only £7 10s, instead of the usual £10, probably because the young doctors thought they were dealing with inexperienced bodysnatchers. They did not ask how the body was obtained, and said 'they would be glad to see them again when they had any other body to dispose of.'

Dr Monro had a fortunate escape. For 'John and William', the names by which they were known to Knox's assistants, were Burke and Hare – William Burke and William Hare – who would bring infamy and ruin to their master.

The first body they had delivered was that of Donald, an army pensioner, who had stayed at Log's Lodgings, a mean hostel in Tanner's Close run by Hare and his self-styled wife, Margaret Laird, an Irishwoman and widow of the previous owner.

Donald had died on 29 November, owing his disgruntled

landlord £4. Hare proposed to Burke they sell the corpse to the doctors and he would get a share of the price. Burke, a cobbler, agreed. He and his Scots common-law wife, Nelly McDougal, were paying guests at the single-storey hovel, where a 'Beds to Let' sign tempted vagrants to part with board money of 3d per night.

Donald's body was lifted out of its coffin and substituted with bark from the nearby tannery. The coffin was nailed down and buried in St Cuthbert's.

On a visit to Greyfriars Churchyard, Robert Louis Stevenson was shown a certain window by a grave-digger where Burke, he was told, had sat 'with pipe and nightcap to watch burials going forward on the green.' But Burke and Hare, even though their neighbours in the West Port might have suspected otherwise, never lifted a body from a graveyard.

After Donald's pitiful body had made them rich – Hare kept £4 5s, and the corpse's shirt, while Burke pocketed £3 5s – they formed a business partnership that would result in mass murder.

Burke and Hare kept no books – and Knox's records were never made public – but it is generally recognised that the pair killed 16 people, in a period covering almost the whole of 1828. When arrested in November that year the number and description of their victims tallied, but the order in which they were killed did not match.

However, it is believed their first victim was Joseph, a miller, and another of Hare's lodgers, who had been poorly. He apparently had family connections with the owners of Carron Iron Works, the Scottish cannon makers. But it was felt Joseph's fever was scaring off lodgers, so Burke and Hare smothered him with his pillow. He fetched £10 from Knox. Whatever the fee, over the coming months Mrs Hare claimed £1 of Burke's share as some sort of poll tax. Burke would later disclose that he refused to stump up the £1 after one murder and Hare's harpy ignored him for three weeks.

Burke and Hare descended into a downward spiral of

booze and brutal murder. The pageant of blood prompted John Wilson, alias Christopher North to write in *Blackwood's Magazine* in March 1829: 'First ae drunk auld wife, and then anither drunk auld wife – and then a third drunk auld wife – and then a drunk auld or sick man or twa. The confession got unco monotonous – the Lights and Shadows o' Scottish death want relief – though, to be sure, poor Peggy Paterson, the Unfortunate, broke in a little on the uniformity; and sae did Daft Jamie.'

Mary Paterson or Mitchell, a bonny, well-rounded prostitute, was the only one of the victims not to be murdered in Tanner's Close. On the night of 8 April, Mary and her friend, Janet Brown, both 18 years old, were arrested (probably for drunkenness or soliciting) and locked up in the Canongate watch-house. At six next morning they were released and immediately made tracks for a nearby pub. They ordered a gill of whisky from Swanson, the landlord, and soon after were approached by an affable Burke.

Burke bought the girls drink, then hoodwinked them into believing he was single and lodged in Gibb's Close in the Canongate. In fact it was the home of his brother Constantine (Con) and his family.

Mary fell dead drunk at the table as the cunning Burke played out a charade for the benefit of Janet, whom he had earmarked for Dr Knox's dissecting table, along with her drunken friend. But Helen McDougal unexpectedly disrupted the drinking session and in a furious row Burke hurled a tumbler at her, cutting her eyebrow. Con Burke, a scavenger for the town council, was at work, and his wife shot off to find Hare, in the hope he would placate the feuding Burkes.

A terrified Janet fled the scene, but at the bidding of a former landlady, Mrs Janet Lawrie, she returned with a maid to bring Mary away.

On her return to Gibb's Close she found only the two Hares and McDougal. Of Burke, there was no sign. Janet was told Burke and Mary had gone out, but she was invited to linger. Unknown to her, the body of her erstwhile friend lay on the bed, her body covered with a sheet. The horrible truth was hidden from her by the bed curtains. Burke had meanwhile hurried off to Dr Knox to clinch a sale. Janet would have certainly joined Mary in Surgeons' Square had not a suspicious Mrs Lawrie again ordered her maid to return to Gibb's Close and fetch her home.

Janet never gave up looking for Mary, and on questioning Con Burke yet again about her friend's disappearance he replied heatedly: 'How the hell can I tell about you sort of folk? You are here today and away tomorrow.'

Prophetic words. Mary Paterson had been put into a tea-box and carried in broad daylight to Dr Knox's dissecting rooms, as urchins chanted: 'They are carrying a corpse.' She was delivered within five or six hours of her murder. In a clenched fist she grasped twopence-halfpenny. Her body fetched £8.

But Fergusson, Knox's assistant, received a nasty jolt. He and a tall lad recognised Mary. On inquiring where they had got the body, Burke said he had bought it from an old woman at the back of the Canongate. Burke borrowed a pair of scissors to cut Mary's flowing hair, no doubt as a perk. Her body attracted a good deal of attention and was kept for three months in whisky. An admiring student wrote: 'Her body could not fail to attract attention by its voluptuous form and beauty; students crowded around the table on which she lay, and artists came to study a model worthy of Phidias and the best Greek art.' A drawing by one of those artists (J. Oliphant) has survived.

The murder of 'Daft Jamie' Wilson, in October 1828, was the second last, and probably the most foul of the crimes of Burke and Hare. Burke claimed that Hare's wife led Jamie to the Hares' hostel like 'a dumb lamb to the slaughter, and as a sheep to the shearers'. After Mrs Hare enticed the 18-year-old simpleton to the lodging house she locked the door on the outside then pushed the key beneath it, then took off.

The inoffensive Jamie was a familiar figure on the streets of the old toon. His father died when he was 12, and his mother hawked wares. Jamie quit the family home after a dispute and fended for himself on the streets, although at the time of his death he lodged in Stevenlaw's Close in the High Street, where, by an ironic twist of criminal history, lived John Dallas, the sickly child 'burked' by Torrance and Waldie in the previous century.

'Daft Jamie' walked with a stoop and had malformed feet. He was the butt of cruel jokes from the very young who challenged him to fight at the least opportunity. Jamie would have none of it and hurry away, tears brimming in his eyes. But he grew in stature after his death, and was the subject of lithographs, ballads and poems.

Jamie, whose constant companion was Bobby Awl, also delighted in simple riddles, such as:

'Tho' I black and dirty am
An' black as black can be;
There's many a lady that will come
An' by the haun' tak' me.

Question: What am I?
Answer: A teapot.

Poor Jamie did not give up his life without a struggle. Burke and Hare gave him whisky to befuddle his senses, but when they pounced the innocent Jamie, who was lying on top of the bed, fought back. Hare clapped one hand over Jamie's mouth and the other over his nose.

As Hare and their victim landed on the floor, Burke threw himself on top of the youth, and seized his hands and feet. They smothered their victim then stripped him. Hare kept the youth's brass snuff box and gave the copper snuff spoon to his accomplice. His clothes were given to Con Burke's offspring. They later agreed that Jamie had shown great courage.

The body of 'Daft Jamie' was recognised by some of the occupants in Dr Knox's rooms, although the eminent surgeon persisted it was not the kenspeckle character. Even so, when word of his disappearance spread, Knox ordered

Jamie's dissection. His head and feet were swiftly removed.

Burke was said to have been haunted by the mounting catalogue of murders. He slept by candlelight, and perhaps found solace in the religious pamphlets he kept, or at the gospel meetings he had attended in the nearby Grassmarket.

One day in June 1828 his glib tongue lured an Irishwoman and her grandson, both visiting from Glasgow, to Tanner's Close. Burke and Hare suffocated the grandmother, and then killed the child, a deaf mute. Burke was supposed to have snapped the boy's spine with his bare hands, but that was unlikely. A body bearing such a terrible injury would have instantly alerted the suspicions of Knox and his colleagues. The bodies were packed in a herring barrel and transported to Surgeons' Square.

The evil partnership split for a short spell. When Burke and Nelly returned from a holiday in Falkirk they discovered Hare had killed an unknown woman. The Burkes went to lodge with the Brogan family in Tanner's Close, and later took over the house when the Brogans left.

Burke would kill by himself on only one occasion. His victim was Peggy Haldane, a prostitute, whose mother, stout Mrs Mary Haldane who had 'but one tooth in her mouth', had been murdered earlier by Burke and Hare in Hare's stable. The partnership was riven by suspicion. Hare's wife urged Burke to kill Nelly because 'they could not trust her, as she was a Scotch woman,' but Burke loved his Nelly too much for that to happen.

But in early autumn 1828 the pair did kill a next of kin. Ann McDougal, a cousin of Nelly's former husband, paid the Burkes a visit. Burke and Hare got the young woman drunk, but Burke hesitated because 'being a distant friend, he did not like to begin first on her.' Hare suffocated her while Burke prevented her from struggling. Knox's helper, Davie Paterson, gave them 'a fine trunk to put her into'.

But time was running out for them. In the last few months before their arrest they believed themselves infallible. 'They might be as well hanged for a sheep as a lamb,' Burke told his confessors. They made it their business to hunt down potential victims. 'It was God's providence that put a stop to their murdering career, or he does not know how far they might have gone with it, even to attack people on the streets, as they were so successful, and always met with a ready market: that when they delivered a body they were always told to get more.'

Burke and Hare toyed with the idea of extending their trade to Glasgow, or even Ireland, but they had become greedy and careless. Their last victim was a middle-aged Irishwoman, Madgy Docherty, who crossed Burke's path when she entered Rymer's grog shop in the West Port, on 31 October 1828. Burke recognised the stranger's accent and on learning her name suggested they might be related. Docherty was invited back to Burke's dwelling and would later join in the Hallowe'en revelry. Burke had murder in mind, and he immediately ordered his lodgers called Gray, and their child, to leave because they were making too much noise. He arranged for them to stay at Hare's, and even paid for their lodgings. Next morning Ann Gray returned to Burke's to collect her child's stockings. There was no sign of Docherty. They were told Docherty had been too friendly with her host and the jealous Nelly had shown her the door. On straying too close to a heap of straw at the foot of the bed Mrs Gray was warned to keep clear.

Mrs Gray's curiosity was stirred, and that evening she and her husband went back. The Burkes and Hares had gone. Mrs Gray lifted the straw and saw Mrs Docherty's dead and naked body. In the passage the Grays bumped into McDougal, who, realising the grim game was up, pleaded with them to hold their tongues. She offered James Gray a bribe of five or six shillings, 'and if he would be quiet, it might be worth ten pounds a week to him.'

The matter was reported to the police but, by the time they arrived at Tanner's Close, the dead woman had vanished. They did find fresh blood on the straw and Docherty's striped bed-gown.

Next morning the police called at 10 Surgeons' Square, where Davie Paterson showed them a tea-chest, delivered the night before by Burke, Hare and a porter. It contained the naked body of a woman, later identified as Mrs Docherty.

The Burkes and Hares denied all knowledge of ever seeing Docherty, alive or dead, but soon wild rumours of the blood-chilling events at Tanner's Close swept Edinburgh.

The mob bayed for the blood of Burke and Hare and their spouses. But because of the lack of concrete proof against the quartet, the Lord Advocate, Sir William Rae, was forced to serve indictments only against Burke and McDougal. Hare turned King's Evidence, and Mrs Hare could not give evidence against her husband and vice versa.

The trial began at the High Court, Edinburgh, on Christmas Eve 1828, with Burke accused of the murders of Mary Paterson, Daft Jamie and Madgy Docherty. McDougal was charged with the murder of the last named.

The court sat without a break for the next twenty-four hours and did not rise until after the Justice Clerk, Lord Boyle, had donned the black cap and passed the death sentence on Burke.

A juror, George Lutenor, a local portrait painter, sketched the chief protagonists in the gripping drama.

The star witness was the grinning Hare, his death's-head features highlighted by candlelight. His evidence put a rope around Burke's neck. He described how Burke murdered Docherty – 'he put one hand under the nose, and the other under her chin, under her mouth' – while he sat watching in a chair.

The indictment against McDougal was found not proven. A relieved Burke told his partner, 'Nelly, you are out of the scrape.'

Lord Boyle sentenced Burke to hanging but decided not to have the condemned man's corpse exhibited in chains, because the sight might offend the public.

Instead, he told Burke: 'I am disposed to agree that your sentence shall be put into execution in the usual way, but accompanied with the statutory attendant of the punishment of the crime of murder, namely that your body should be publicly dissected and anatomised. And I trust, that if it is ever customary to preserve skeletons, yours will be preserved, in order that posterity may keep in remembrance your atrocious crimes.'

The public never tired of reading about the West Port murders. The *Edinburgh Evening Courant* sold more than 8,000 extra copies. There was a great outcry that many key witnesses, including Dr Knox and three of his assistants, were never called to give evidence. The family of Daft Jamie failed to bring a private prosecution of murder against Hare.

But the biggest talking point was Burke's two confessions, both given in the condemned cell at the Calton Jail. The first, known as the 'official' version was dictated in the presence of a sheriff and other legal officials. The *Courant* confession, which was much more revealing, was obtained by an enterprising reporter. Burke exonerated Knox of all knowledge of the crimes. It was published after the hanging.

Burke, weighed down by iron fetters and bouts of guilt, reflected on his past life as a soldier, he was a batman in the Donegal Militia, and how he left his wife and family in Ireland for construction work on the Union Canal, connecting the Forth and Clyde Canal in Falkirk to Port Hopetoun, Edinburgh. He was also a weaver and a baker before learning to mend shoes in Leith. Hare too was a navvy on the Union but they did not meet until Hallowfair in November 1827. Within a year they had murdered sixteen people. Burke was born in Urney, County Tyrone, in 1792, while Hare, claimed to be 25 and a native of Armagh.

On Wednesday, 28 January 1829, Burke walked the few steps from the lock-up in Libberton's Wynd, where he had spent a restless night, to the scaffold in the Lawnmarket. A vast crowd, estimated to be 25,000, howled their hate from street level to the roof tops. 'Burke him!', they screamed, and so added a new verb to the English language. 'Hare! Hare! Bring out Hare!' 'Hang Knox!' they yelled.

Burke spoke briefly on the drop. Hangman Thomas Williams was adjusting the rope when Burke reminded him that the knot of his neck-kerchief was behind him. (On his death in 1833 Williams would be succeeded by his son.)

Burke died almost without a struggle. After 40 minutes his body was cut down, placed in a coffin, and carried to the lock-up. The hangman and his assistants scrambled to get portions of the rope while the crowd had to settle for shavings from the coffin.

Overnight the body was removed to Dr Monro's rooms in the College for dissection next day. Hundreds queued for admission.

Tickets were issued to only VIPs and regular students, but other students, angry at the lock-out, smashed windows of the anatomical theatre in frustration. The police hit out with their batons. Peace was restored after Robert Christison, Professor of Medical Jurisprudence, who had given medical evidence at the trial, suggested they be allowed inside. Christison estimated that 40,000 persons filed past the partly dissected body during the next two days.

Burke's accomplice, Hare, and their respective spouses made themselves scarce. Mrs Hare, clutching her infant, was pelted with snowballs and stones after being released from the Calton Jail, and had to be rescued by the police. In Glasgow the unhappy woman was again attacked by a mob and she was once again locked up for her own security. She was sent down to Greenock where she boarded a steamboat for Belfast – and obscurity.

On 5 February 1829, after a last-gasp bid by Daft Jamie's mother and sister to sue Hare for £500 came to naught, William Hare, travelling under the name of 'Mr Black', caught the southbound mail. At Noblehouse, the second stage of the journey, the coach stopped for supper. Hare, who had been an outside passenger, sat at the back of the inn with his hat on and his face muffled by his cloak. But when invited to heat himself at the fire he took off his hat, and was recognised by E. Douglas Sandford, the counsel who had acted for the Wilsons during their unsuccessful action against Hare.

Hare climbed into a vacant 'inside' seat when the journey resumed, but a disgusted Sandford ordered him out. The outcast went back to the top of the coach, and by the time it reached Dumfries his identity was known. News of Hare's arrival in Dumfries spread, and the editor of the *Dumfries Courier* was roused from his bed. Hare took refuge in the tap-room of the King's Arms Inn, where initial friendliness towards him – he was even bought drinks – turned to frustration when he refused to talk about his crimes, saying he had done his duty in Edinburgh. Outside a crowd of 8,000 packed High Street – 'so closely wedged, that you might have almost walked over their heads' – as Hare waited to catch the coach to Portpatrick, and a boat to his homeland.

As the mood of the crowd grew nastier both inside and outside the King's Arms, the police arrived in force. Hare faced a lynch mob that would have willingly hanged him from a post or drowned him in the Nith. What was to be done? The passengers were sent off in two gigs ahead of the coach, which resumed its journey with great difficulty. The mob believed Hare was hiding inside the boot. The gates at the Gassylands toll-bar were barricaded by locals and the coach searched. But the morose Hare was still a prisoner in the King's Arms, where it was reported, a doctor had prevented him from 'letting the mob 'tak' their will o' him.'

A decoy chaise was brought to the door of the inn and a trunk buckled on with much fuss. In a well-planned manoeuvre, Hare jumped out of a back window and leapt into another chaise, which was driven at great speed to the jail.

The mob, furious they had been cheated of their quarry, vented their anger on the courthouse and jail. But first they extinguished street gas lamps, presumably so that they would not be identified. Windows were smashed among other acts of vandalism. One hundred special constables were sworn in, and rushed to the scene wielding batons. There was talk of burning down the jail, and mounting attacks on the homes of local doctors. In the early hours of the following morning Hare was escorted through empty streets to the edge of Dumfries. Because the whole of population of

Galloway were in arms, and stages to Portpatrick were being searched, he was shown the road to Annan. He was spotted by a boy at three in the morning at Dodbeck. The driver of a mail coach recognised him sitting beside two stone-breakers on the public road within half-a-mile of Carlisle – despite Hare holding down his head to prevent recognition. The last sighting was the next morning, a Sunday, at a small village two miles beyond Carlisle.

Burke's stumpy skeleton remains in the Anatomy Museum at Edinburgh University, but, of Hare, there was no trace. He is supposed to have roamed the streets of London a blind beggar, as a result of being thrown into a lime pit by avenging townsfolk.

A fanciful tale from Perthshire suggested Hare was the real identity of a centenarian Irish peddler who sold his wares at Aberfeldy railway station!

But what of Dr Knox? The colourful career of the brilliant anatomist was destroyed by the Burke and Hare scandal. At the beginning of October 1828 he promised budding doctors an ample supply of anatomical subjects over the winter session. He paid nearly £800 from his own pocket to supply bodies, and in 1828 five hundred pupils enrolled in his extra-mural classes.

Youngsters chanted, 'Hang Burke, banish Hare; Burn Knox in Surgeons' Square'. A large crowd of their elders attempted to burn his effigy outside the surgeon's home in Newington. The dummy, recognisable in gaudy waistcoat and bearing a placard, 'Knox, the associate of the infamous Hare', was torn to shreds instead. Knox, who had attended the wounded of Waterloo, was no coward. With the mob baying for his blood at his front door, he left by the back to keep a dinner appointment. Knox was prepared for trouble, having armed himself with a sword, pistols and a dirk. On his safe arrival he told his host: 'You see my arms, and had I been called upon to defend myself, I would have measured a score of the brutes.'

In Newington, police could not prevent the mob from vandalising his garden and breaking the windows of his house. Knox, despite his brave front, became a reviled figure.

The *Edinburgh Evening Chronicle* thundered: 'In purchasing the bodies which had come under the fell gripe of the Burkes and Hares, there must have been an utter recklessness, a thorough indifference, as to the causes and consequences, which, in point of criminality, very closely borders upon guilty knowledge.' The same newspaper did not spare its punches when it claimed 'the agitation of public feeling will never subside till the city be released of this man's presence, or until his innocence be manifested. In justice to himself, if he is innocent, in justice to the public, if he is guilty, he ought to be put on trial.'

In March 1829 a committee which investigated the allegations against Knox published its findings. It had been under the chairmanship of the Marquis of Queensferry but he had resigned for some unknown reason. Sir Walter Scott refused to join it, because did not wish to 'lend a hand to whitewash this much to be suspected individual. But he shall ride off on no back of mine.'

The committee found no evidence that Knox or his assistants had any knowledge of the murders, but thought the anatomist had acted in a 'very incautious manner' in his dealings with the murderers.

In the years that followed, Knox's classes began to dwindle. He was hounded out of Edinburgh, and, in Glasgow in 1844, his classes were so small he gave his students their fees back. He died in shabby-gentility in Hackney, London, in 1862.

In his memoirs Christison believed Knox had 'rather wilfully shut his eyes to incidents which ought to have excited the grave suspicions of a man of his intelligence.' Christison, who gave medical evidence at Burke's trial, added: 'Knox, a man of undoubted talent, but notoriously deficient in principle and in heart, was exactly the person to blind himself against suspicion, and fall into blameable carelessness. But it was absurd to charge him with anything worse.'

Chapter 8
Mob Rule

The bleak, sinister-looking building in Hospital Row was an accursed sight to the deeply superstitious of Aberdeen who had given it the scurrilous title of the 'Burkin' Hoose'.

It bore three 'false, church-looking windows' to discourage snoopers and the only daylight leaked through windows at the back of the building and a glass dome on the roof.

The brand-new Aberdeen Anatomical Theatre, run by 'clever, dirty Andrew Moir' (see Chapter 2), was built because of the generosity of several influential friends. He delivered his first lecture there in November 1831.

Moir, of course, had not escaped the wrath of the general public during the Burke and Hare scandal. In 1829, a sack containing a limbless corpse of a man stolen from New Deer, Aberdeenshire, was abandoned near Moir's previous premises in the Guestrow. The *Aberdeen Journal* warned: 'We had occasion before to caution resurrectionists not to tamper with the present and provoked state of public feeling; for some dreadful and summary mode of punishment will unquestionably overtake those who engage in such wanton and outrageous acts.'

In March, a month after Burke's execution, word got round that a stolen body was being dissected in Moir's rooms. A mob attacked the building, tearing off windows shutters, smashing furniture and destroying surgical instruments. A man tried to wrench the slates off the roof as others started a bonfire in the street. The town sergeants and police broke up the disturbance and one man was arrested. A subsequent search revealed a body which was taken to Drum's Aisle in nearby St Nicholas Church.

There was a rumour that a box filled with human skulls had been found in Moir's rooms.

But resentment against Moir died down, and, with an

upsurge in students enrolling in his extra-mural studies, he looked for more suitable premises.

But by the end of 1831 the 'burkers' were again in the news. On 5 December John Bishop and Thomas Williams, (real name Head), were hanged at Newgate amid disgraceful crowd scenes. They were dubbed the 'London Burkers' for they had drowned their drugged victims in a garden well then sold their corpses. Jack May, who, like Bishop and Williams, earned his living as a resurrectionist, was respited, but died soon after. Bishop confessed that the Burke and Hare case had given them the idea to murder.

The *Aberdeen Journal* ran a report of the execution. On the same page a smaller item, headed 'Supposed Attempt at Burking', claimed two boys were approached in the street by two well-dressed and rather young men, who asked them to run an errand for which they would be well rewarded. The boys followed the men into John Street but ran off when the strangers began whispering to each other.

'This is the boys' simple statement, and the readers may make any comment on it they choose,' declared the newspaper.

Neighbours who lived near Hospital Row, a rough track that crossed a bleaching green near the west end of St Andrew Street, had already complained that the new building was a source of an intolerable stench.

The combination of the Newgate execution and the alleged attempted abduction of the boys near Aberdeen's unpopular 'Burkin' Hoose', led to violence against Dr Moir and his anatomical theatre on the afternoon of Monday, 19 December 1831.

It began with a dog sniffing and scraping in the loose earth behind the building. The dog tugged at something. Curious children and young tannery workers pressed forward. To their horror the dog had revealed the mangled portions of a human body that had been improperly buried. They raised the alarm and a crowd gathered.

Dr Moir prepared to deliver a lecture when the back door of the theatre was forced open, and the crowd invaded his class. Moir and his students withdrew to a smaller room as they were beaten and kicked. They were forced to lock the door as the fury of the mob grew. Moir and his students slipped out of an unguarded exit. The anatomist was recognised and chased through the streets. He ran along Crooked Lane and down Schoolhill before reaching the safety of his rooms in the Guestrow.

At the 'Burkin' Hoose' meantime the mob burst into a dissecting room and found three dead bodies stretched out on wooden boards. They were in various states of dissection; one had half its skull removed. The bodies were carried on makeshift stretchers to Drum's Aisle. No attempt was made to cover the cadavers as they passed through a crowd, growing uglier by the minute. 'Burn the hoose! Down with the Burkin' shop!' they screamed, and attempts began to set fire to the building.

In the Guestrow a crowd bayed for Moir's blood outside number 63. His front window panes were knocked in. Moir slipped from a back window to give protesters the slip.

The sky to the west glowed red. Flames danced in the blood-shot smoke. The anatomical theatre was ablaze, fuelled by mason's timber, shavings and tar barrels. The fury of the mob mounted. Using stout planks as levers they began to undermine the walls.

Provost James Hadden appeared on the scene with magistrates, town sergeants and a posse of special policeman, called the Day Patrole. He tried to placate the crowd by assuring them that every inquiry would be made, and every satisfaction afforded, if any crime had been committed by Dr Moir. By now a crowd of between ten and twenty thousand people, almost half the population of the city, was squeezed into surroundings streets, cheering, chanting and shouting. Provost Hadden warned them of the serious penalties they could face and made a half-hearted attempt to read the Riot Act, the last time this was done in Aberdeen, but his words were lost in the loud cheering. Tongues of fire licked the 'Burkin' Hoose'. Dr Moir's dreams were going up in smoke.

Fearful that the rioters might spread the conflagration to other public buildings in the area, such as the Medical Society's Hall, the magistrates called out the troops at Castlehill Barracks.

Two hours after the inquisitive mongrel found the body-parts the fire brigade appeared – only to find no water could be obtained for their hoses.

But even if water had been at hand, the rioters told the firemen they would not be allowed to douse the fire.

Soldiers of the 79th Cameron Highlanders played no part in quelling the riot. They were marched into the grounds of Gordon's Hospital by a far gate where they remained on stand-by till the end of the trouble. A second detachment guarded Schoolhill. There was good reason for their inactivity; on the last occasion the army dealt with troublemakers in Aberdeen there was bloodshed. The Ross and Cromarty Rangers, campaign-hardened troops fresh from quelling Irish rebels, fired on an unarmed crowd, killing four persons, and wounding at least ten, during George III's birthday celebrations in the Castlegate on 4 June 1802.

Provost Hadden, who faced the 'Burkin' Hoose' mob almost 30 years later, had forced the troops to return to their barracks after ordering the arrest of their officer.

The back wall of the 'Burkin' Hoose' was pushed over by the mob; next they undermined the front wall, with a little more effort. The roof and gables formed a blazing arch, until the roof collapsed with a fierce roar amidst a cloud of sparks. Dr Moir's anatomical theatre was reduced to a smouldering ruin by eight o'clock at night.

For the next few hours the crowd played hare-and-hounds with any young student rash enough to go outdoors. One was recognised and chased by a crowd yelling, 'A Burker! A Burker, doon with the bloody rascal!' He was severely manhandled before the police intervened. It was said Dr Moir spent the night hidden under a tablestone in St Nicholas Kirkyard.

Three men who were arrested during the riot appeared

at the Circuit Court in Aberdeen on 24 April 1832. Alexander Murray, flesher, of West North Street and George Sharpe, of Schoolhill, both Aberdeen, and Alexander Allan, a private in the Fusilier Guards, were charged with mobbing and rioting, wilful fire-raising and assault. The Advocate-Depute said because of the extenuating circumstances, and that the incident appeared to have been due to carelessness on part of the medical men accepted a modified plea of mobbing and rioting, and dropped the capital charge of wilful fire-raising. Charges of assaulting Dr Moir and a student, James Polson, were also dropped.

The court accepted that the accused were not the ringleaders. Sharpe claimed he had gone to the theatre to see if he could find the body of his grandmother who had been buried a few weeks earlier. They were each jailed for twelve months, to be served in a less harsh jail.

Furious arguments raged over the handling of the riot by the town council and the police. Francis Clerihew, a local advocate and friend of the doctors, who supplemented his income by writing for the *Aberdeen Monthly Magazine*, pointed out that respectable taxpayers would have to 'pay for this frolic of the mob and Magistracy.' In his youth, Clerihew, who became a Sheriff-Substitute, undoubtedly joined his medical friends on bodysnatching forays. His fictional story, *My First Resurrection*, has the ring of truth.

A careless porter was blamed for burying body-parts in the backyard of the anatomical theatre. The disposal of human remains violated the senses of the general public. Knox and other Edinburgh anatomists had dissected corpses buried at Greyfriars. Aberdeen bodysnatchers were rumoured to have buried dismembered bodies in a wood at Gillahill Farm, near the Lang Stracht.

Dr Moir became a figure of notoriety. His house was pelted with rotten vegetables and dead hens, and its lantern torn down by youths and kicked like a football along the cobbled street.

After Moir and his backers won damages of £235 from the town council over the destruction of the anatomical theatre, he gradually rebuilt his shattered career. He was soon lecturing in new rooms to packed classes.

In 1839, he wed his childhood sweetheart, Agnes Fraser. In the same year he was appointed lecturer in anatomy at a medical school close by King's College, Aberdeen. But in 1844, at the early age of 38, he contracted typhoid fever from a patient and died. Three days later his wife gave birth to their first child. Moir is buried under a crumbling table tombstone in St Nicholas Kirkyard, where 13 years before he had hidden from a marauding mob.

One of the earliest anti-resurrectionist riots in 19th-century Scotland took place in Glasgow.

In January 1803, the theft of a woman's body from the new burial ground at the High Church sparked two days of rioting. The target of the rioters was the Old College. On 25 January, the *Glasgow Courier* reported how a disorderly crowd had gathered at the gates of the college while magistrates conducted a search of all the rooms. But despite assurances by the magistrates the crowd knocked in almost all the front windows of the building, and threatened to force entry. There were no casualties but a number of troublemakers were arrested.

A company of soldiers was hired to guard the college to allow classes to carry on.

The same edition of the *Courier* published notices offering rewards in connection with the theft of the body, and the subsequent riot. The magistrates offered 20 guineas for information leading to the arrest and conviction of any person or persons responsible for the theft, while James Hill, the college factor, offered 100 guineas for the arrest and conviction of those responsible for demolishing the college windows. The college senate ordered a lecturer in anatomy to quit his rooms in the college, while his students were threatened with expulsion if they were found to be implicated in grave-robbing.

In February 1822 Glasgow was the scene of a riot blamed on bodysnatching activity. A mob ransacked the home of oil and colour merchant George Provand in the mistaken belief it was a den of resurrectionists. The uproar raged for hours before the Riot Act was read, and troops summoned to keep order.

Five people were found guilty after trial in the High Court and each transported overseas for 14 years. The ringleader, John Campbell, a shoemaker, formerly a policeman, was flogged at the tail of a cart through the streets of Glasgow by Tammas Young, the public hangman. The first 20 strokes were inflicted outside the jail. The dose was repeated twice at either end of the Stockwell, with the last 20, making 80 strokes in all, inflicted before a huge crowd at Glasgow Cross.

In Scotland, and elsewhere in Britain, at the end of 1831, the days of the bodysnatchers and disciples of Burke and Hare, were numbered. The public were sickened beyond belief by the blood-chilling revelations from Tanner's Close and Bethnal Green, the haunt of the London Burkers.

In Lanarkshire a gang of resurrectionists took refuge in an inn with their captors, the fiscal and police, after a woman's body they had stolen from Carluke was found in a shallow grave near Wishaw. They were smuggled on horseback to jail in Lanark as the public vented their rage on a gig abandoned by the bodysnatchers. At Kirkintilloch, near Glasgow, a farmer set his hounds on four men attempting to lift a body from the Old Isle graveyard.

At Inveresk, near Musselburgh, two medical students were collared while attempting to lift a body from the churchyard. They were held in a private house but asked to be locked up in jail for they feared for their lives. Sure enough an angry crowd, armed with axes and other implements, surrounded the jail. The pair survived to appear before the Sheriff, and they were later liberated on bail.

It was the year the great Reform Bill began its roller-coaster passage through Parliament and the Lords, and Henry Warburton, MP for Bridport, introduced his new Anatomy Bill.

But before the new Anatomy Act became reality (it

received Royal Assent on 1 August 1832) Paisley was rocked by ugly riots.

The Renfrewshire town was in the grip of a cholera epidemic and a rumour was spread that the doctors were adopting a plan of killing people by introducing cholera among them, and burying the bodies where they could be easily obtained.

The first cholera victim, Murdoch Galbreath, a hawker, died at his home in the town's New Sneddon Street on 13 February 1832. In four days nine out of 18 persons who contracted cholera died. The sick were confined in Hutchison's Charity School, Oakshaw Street, now part of the Holy Trinity Church hall. The poor, unlike the better-off, had no graveyard of their own, so magistrates opened a new burial ground at the Moss Lands, close to the Greenock Road toll-bar, near the present-day St James Park.

On Sunday, 19 February, a party of labourers employed by the local Board of Health called at McFarlane's Close, New Sneddon Street, to bury the body of a boy. No sooner had the men arrived by cart than a crowd of locals turned out brandishing knives and pokers, and, swearing by the powers 'that the devil a bit of the body should the Burking spalpeens be allowed to touch'. (A 'spailpeen' was Irish slang for an itinerant worker).

The attempt to bury the boy was abandoned, but after the re-commencement of the burial service the labourers returned. They managed to remove the coffin and the cart moved off, mobbed by the angry crowd. A cry rang out: 'Ye may be after taking him, but before ye's reach the moss, every man and mother's son of ye's will be Burked, and chucked in the same hole!' Missiles showered down on the labourers as the yelling crowd surged around the cart.

At the west end of St James' Street the horse was seized and the coffin borne in triumph back to McFarlane's Close.

The Sheriff, procurator-fiscal and several magistrates, backed by a force of police officers, arrived on the scene in the afternoon. After the Sheriff had warned the crowd about their conduct the coffin was allowed safe passage to the

Moss, where it was buried in front of the lawmen and several thousand spectators.

The health authority acted swiftly to try and stop the spread of the disease. A curfew on late-night drinking was introduced, and the streets and lanes were fumigated with diluted sulphuric acid and chloride of lime. In some neighbourhoods flaming tar barrels were placed opposite houses where there had been cases of cholera. A notice with the word, 'Sick', was posted on doors and closes where patients lived.

Fear of the bodysnatchers was not far from the thoughts of the poor. A father assaulted a doctor who was tending his sick son at their home in Storie Street, under the mistaken belief his son was being deliberately infected.

The magistrates ordered the man to pay a fine of £5, or face three weeks behind bars. In Glasgow, there were arrests after a cholera riot in the Gorbals, during which a surgeon, magistrates and police were attacked. One offender was sent to the Bridewell for 60 days on a diet of bread of water.

In Paisley, the persecution of the doctors intensified, and it was firmly believed they were allowing empty coffins to be buried in the Moss and were selling the bodies.

If the Aberdeen 'Burkin' Hoose' rampage was started by an inquisitive dog, the second, and by far the worst Paisley riot, was also due to an accidental find.

On 26 March, a Sabbath, some persons strolling near the Moss burial ground found two shovels and a cord with an iron hook attached. According to the *Paisley Advertiser:* 'These to the finders were irrefragable proof that the resurrectionists had been committing depredations.'

The implements were brought back to the town and exhibited next day in a shop in Blacklaw Lane. A large crowd gathered in the district before rushing off to the Moss to determine the truth of the grave-robbing rumours. One of the first coffins exhumed was found to be empty! Eye-witnesses spread reports in town that of eight coffins lifted only one contained a body. The crowd was in an ugly mood. The empty coffin was carried shoulder-high to the town.

The posts which fenced the ground were torn up and 'shouldered like a forest of pikes', as the mob, 'breathing destruction to the doctors' marched in growing strength towards Paisley.

An effort was made by Provost William Gilmour, Sheriff-Substitute Campbell, magistrates and the captain of police, to cool the hot-heads. In Glen Lane, the coffin was taken from its bearers and broken, and many of those brandishing fence posts tossed the weapons aside in shame. But ironic shouts of 'hurrah for the doctors!' infuriated the crowd. The police were attacked and one withdrew to the safety of a house which instantly had its windows riddled with stones. The mob now turned their wrath on the town's medical men, attacking the shops or houses of twelve doctors, including surgeons, and a prominent member of the Board of Health.

In Oakshaw Street they forced open the gates of the cholera hospital, and smashed 50 panes of glass. Two men broke into the building and terrorised the dying patients. The cholera hearse was seized by the mob and dragged to the canal with the intention to throw it in, but it was decided the procession would be less impressive without it. By now the hearse been reduced to the wheels and its shafts.

At Paisley Cross an official group, headed by a bailie, pleaded with the crowd, who surrendered the skeletal hearse before retreating across the Old Bridge. Soon after two troops of cavalry had arrived from Glasgow the trouble died down and they withdrew. A dense throng milling in front of the County Buildings also melted into the background.

Some surgeons felt the riot had been instigated by their enemies, pointing to the fact an empty coffin should have been in the grave first exhumed. It was only two feet below the surface, and, unlike the coffins of cholera victims, was untarred.

That evening nine coffins were raised at the Moss, but none had been desecrated. For the first time an official watch was mounted to deter any bodysnatchers. The next day the remainder of the coffins were disinterred, when it was found two more bodies were missing.

A bid was made to bring the empty coffins into town but that was prevented. Handbills were circulated offering a reward of £50 for the discovery of the resurrectionists.

The riots shocked the respectable burghers of Paisley who criticised the 'brutal and savage passions' of the 'lawless mob.' At their meeting on 28 March the Board of Health reluctantly accepted the collective resignation from public duties by the town's doctors, including those whose windows were smashed.

It was estimated that the damage caused by the riots was £130. In May 1832, seven Paisley men pleaded guilty at the Court of Justiciary in Glasgow, to charges of mobbing and rioting. The prisoners' counsel attributed the cause to the violation of the graves at the Moss, rather than outrageous feeling towards the town's surgeons. Two of the accused had relatives buried there. The culprits were sent to the Paisley Bridewell. Joseph Green and Christopher Welsh were locked up for nine months; Thomas Forrester, Philip Docherty Peter Mulheran and Thomas Shearer for six months, and John Cumming for three months. John Peacock failed to appear and was outlawed, while James Hunter pleaded not guilty and was sent for trial.

But this was not the first time bodysnatchers had raided Paisley.

On the morning of 8 December 1828, the body of a young woman buried four days before in the burial ground of the United Associate Church in Oakshaw, was stolen. The snatchers were probably disturbed for the grave had only been half-filled.

A young local man approached the girl's father with a queer tale. He claimed that in the early hours of the morning he had overheard suspicious noises in a garret above his house in the town's Back Sneddon district. He suggested it should be searched. The father, accompanied by a policeman, went to the garret, and found his daughter's body in a sack.

Efforts to trace the pillagers of the grave failed, but those of a suspicious nature would have suspected the young man knew more about the incident than he was prepared to say.

Cholera lingered in Paisley till autumn 1832, by which time the death roll reached 446.

It did not restrict itself to the poor quarter of the town. One Monday in October Mrs Todd, the tobacconist's wife, was serving customers in the morning, and by early evening she was dead. Mr Lymburn, cloth merchant, and late senior bailie, took ill the same evening at a meeting of the Old Weavers' Society, and died next day. Hours later his wife expired. The local newspaper reported they had both become 'tenants of the tomb', but gave no details of its location. They, too, would have been buried on the Moss.

Chapter 9
Gothic Mystery

On the cold, wet morning of Thursday, 1 December, 1881, building labourer William Hadden rounded the corner of the Gothic chapel at Dunecht House in Aberdeenshire and stumbled upon a macabre mystery that would horrify Queen Victoria and her nation and reawaken memories of the bodysnatchers.

An iron railing which enclosed the family crypt had been damaged, a layer of soil shovelled off and the huge granite block concealing the only entrance to the tomb was propped open by pieces of wood. Nearby lay two shovels and a pickaxe.

At first Hadden believed his workmates had left a job unfinished, but he was wrong.

The estate commissioner, William Yeats, an Aberdeen advocate, was contacted by telegram and he hurried to Dunecht, 12 miles west of the city, accompanied by Inspector George Cran of Aberdeen Constabulary. They were joined at the grey granite mansion by Constable John Robb, the local policeman from nearby Echt.

The mausoleum under the new chapel, which is Dunecht House's most stunning feature, had space for 64 coffins arranged in tiers. But only one body had been interred – Alexander William Lindsay, born 1812, had succeeded to the title in 1869 as 8th Earl of Balcarres and 25th Earl of Crawford.

Because of ill-health, the Earl of Crawford, a distinguished astronomer, theologian, antiquarian and genealogist, had wintered in Egypt and in Italy, where he died in Florence on 13 December 1880. His embalmed body was placed in three coffins.

The inner coffin was made of soft Italian wood; the middle one of lead; and the outer fashioned of highly-polished, carved oak and mounted with ornate silver. The three coffins were then deposited inside a massive walnut shell, bearing a carving of a cross in high relief. The total weight of all four coffins was almost half-a-ton!

Because the old vault beneath the Lindsay family chapel at Wigan Parish Church in Lancashire was full it was decided the late earl would be interred at Dunecht House. His body was conveyed across the Alps under the care of a trusted family retainer. When the huge coffin left a French port it was lashed to the heaving deck of a specially chartered steamer in an English Channel storm.

Once it had arrived safely in Scotland the earl's body was transported by road from Aberdeen to Dunecht. But, because no hearse was big enough to carry the load, the outer shell had to be removed. It was eventually placed in the vault beside the earl's body, encased within the three coffins. A violent snowstorm swept Scotland, and the hearse was trapped in drifts for several days on the journey back to Aberdeen.

On the cusp of the New Year, the Episcopal Bishop of Aberdeen consecrated the white marble mortuary chapel, and it took eight men to lift the coffin into a niche in the wall. Four heavy slabs of Caithness granite were laid across the short flight of steps leading from the entrance of the tomb to the crypt floor. A granite stone, measuring six feet by four feet, sealed the vault.

It was believed that no one else had set foot in the vault since the interment, but a year later Inspector Cran, lighted candle in hand, was given a nasty shock when he descended the eight steps to the crypt. He shouted on Constable Robb and Yeats to follow. The tools that lay at the entrance of the tomb belonged to the labourers carrying out building work, and had been left in a shed the previous night. On the stairs they almost fell over three iron bars and two planks, but they were unprepared for the horrifying sight of the desecrated tomb. The floor of the vault was strewn with planks and sawdust, and three coffins, which had been dumped on their side and opened.

The Earl of Crawford's body had been stolen!

The vault was filled with the smell of scented sawdust.

The sawdust, it was noted, was mildewed and the leaden shell had turned rusty where it had been hacked open. The police realised some considerable period had elapsed since the actual theft.

Inspector Cran had barely recovered from the grim discovery when he received another shock. Yeats admitted he had been told of the macabre theft almost three months earlier!

On 8 September 1881, Yeats had received an anonymous letter with an Aberdeen postmark. It read: 'Sir – The remains of the late Earl of Crawford are not beneath the chaple (sic) at Dunecht as you believe, but were removed hence last spring, and the smell of decayed flowers ascending from the vault since that time will, on investigation, be found to proceed from another cause than flowers.' It was signed, 'NABOB'.

Yeats had discussed the letter with the builder of the vault and decided it was a wicked hoax. But he had the good sense not to destroy it. The lawyer told Cran that at the end of May he had received reports of a strong odour wafting up from the vault. The housekeeper who had passed the vault on her way to church described it as a 'pleasantly aromatic'. Next day a gardener had noticed the odour which he blamed on decaying wreaths left in the crypt. A crack between flagstones was thought to have been caused by frost and was filled with lime and cement. The crypt was not reopened and instead the area was covered with soil, sown with grass and the iron railing erected.

It was plain the earl's body had not been stolen for medical research. Whoever had committed the theft hoped to hold the body for ransom. The bizarre plot was not original. In 1876 a gang of American counterfeiters had made a daring, but fruitless bid to steal the body of Abraham Lincoln from his tomb. Two years later the body of New York millionaire merchant, Mr T. A. Stewart, was stolen, but, despite his widow's offer to pay the ransom, it was never recovered.

Detectives investigating the Dunecht mystery reasoned

that when the earl's family took no action on receiving the letter from 'Nabob', someone had returned to desecrate the vault again so that the crime would be discovered.

Queen Victoria sent an 'expression of sympathy' to the new peer and his family.

The *Aberdeen Evening Express* commented: 'Body-snatching, though common enough in this as in other districts some 50 years ago, is a crime now almost unknown; and the horror raised by this sacrilegious act is, if anything, deepened by the skill, patience, and masterly villainy that seems to have been brought to bear in its conception and execution.'

A wide-scale search of the 70-acre Dunecht policies and surrounding countryside, involved more that 100 police and estate workers. A guard was mounted on the big house. Searchers were hampered by a severe snowstorm.

The gossip-mongers had a field day. It was whispered that the earl's body had been stolen in Italy; that the family themselves were responsible so as to give them an excuse to sell their Scottish estate; that the dark deed had been the work of Italian decorators working on the Dunecht chapel, and the body shipped back to Florence. Even a newspaper reporter was suspected.

The only real clue police had at this stage was that someone with inside knowledge of the Dunecht estate was to blame. The mysterious 'Nabob' was their prime suspect when further letters arrived, threatening destruction of the earl's body unless £6,000 was paid to the letter writer.

But they were certain that more than one person was implicated. It was impossible for one man alone to uproot the three coffins from their niche in the crypt. Attempts were made to contact the anonymous letter-writer, with appeals in the local press pleading: 'Nabob. Please communicate at once.'

A further appeal, sweetened with a £50 reward for more information, resulted in this inexpertly penned letter:

'Sir, The late Earl of Crawford. The body is still in Aberdeenshire, and I can put you in possession of the same as soon as you bring one or more of the desperados who stole it to justice so that I may know with whom I have to deal. I have no wish to be assinated by rusarectionests, nor suspected by the public of being an accomplice in such dastardly work, which I most assuredly would be unless the gulty party are brought to justice. Had Mr. Yeats acted on the hint I gave him last Sept., he might have found the remains as though by axedand and hunted up the robers at lsure, but that chance is lost, so I hope you will find your men and make it safe and prudent for me to find what you want. P.S. – Should they find out thad an outsider knows their secret it may be removed to another place. NABOB.'

On the advice of the Home Secretary the deceased's family refused to offer a reward for the recovery of his body. Instead, a £600 reward – £500 from the family and £100 from the government – and a free pardon to any accomplice, other than the perpetrator, was offered for information leading to the arrest of the culprit.

The general public never tired of the Dunecht mystery. There was always something new to keep their curiosity alive. A bloodhound called 'Morgan' provided a farcical diversion when his trainer, Mr Spencer of Wigan, brought him to Dunecht to search for the missing corpse.

Morgan, described by the press as the 'famous sleuth hound', had earned his reputation in Blackburn, Lancashire, in March 1876, when he found the remains of a seven-year-old girl, Emily Holland, and helped put the hangman's noose around the neck of her murderer, William Fish, a barber.

Mr Spencer boasted of his dog's exploits in capturing two burglars. 'We started at seven, and by half-past eleven the thieves had got three months apiece.' But Morgan failed to perform in Dunecht Woods. At the curt command, 'Seek, dead!', the 'sagacious' sleuth hound, which had been given the pungent whiff of sawdust used in packing the earl's body, dashed after rabbits. Undeterred, the Aberdeen public queued to pay the sixpence (2.5p) admission to the annual dog show to see the 'famous Morgan'.

The public also had its own theories for solving the mystery. These ranged from conjuring up psychic forces through mediums, to all sorts of useless and time-wasting advice. Peter Castle, an Aberdeen wine merchant described himself as an 'amateur detective'. He took an obsessive interest in the case and actually got himself hired by the new earl. Castle enlisted the help of local clairvoyant, Donald Christie, who claimed the missing body was hidden in St Margaret's Episcopal Church in Aberdeen's Gallowgate. Christie's strange behaviour alarmed the sisters and police were called to eject him. The public ridiculed Christie, nicknaming him, 'The Dunecht Dreamer'. Castle, too, became a figure of fun after his tip-off led to the wrongful arrest of two men, and his effigy was burned by a jeering crowd on April Fool's Day.

The suspected men were Thomas Kirkwood, a joiner employed at Dunecht Estate, and John Philip, a shoemaker, and drill instructor of the Echt Volunteer Corps. Both were released. Philip who was suspected of being 'Nabob' later gave evidence at the trial of the accused.

The mystery took a sensational turn on 18 July 1882 when the earl's body was found swathed in blankets in a shallow grave, 500 yards from the window of his favourite study at Dunecht House. It was located after an eight-hour search in the course of an old ditch, close by a gravel pit, by police and gamekeepers using iron probes.

On the previous day police had arrested Charles Soutar, a 42-year-old rat catcher, of Donald's Court in Schoolhill, in central Aberdeen. Soutar had worked for the Lindsays for five or six years but he was sacked for poaching three years before the earl died.

Police had been tipped off by Aberdeen game dealer George Machray, who had been a gamekeeper at Urie, Stonehaven, when Soutar had worked there as a rat-catcher. Machray had gone to the police following meetings with Soutar who hinted at having inside knowledge of the crime. At one meeting in an Aberdeen pub Soutar asked Machray to act as a go-between with the earl's agent so that he 'could tell where the body was on two conditions, namely that they would find out the persons who took the body, and give protection to him.'

On the day of his arrest Soutar was judicially examined by Sheriff Comrie Thomson in Aberdeen and admitted he had written the 'Nabob' letters.

On being asked; 'What do you know of the removal of the late Earl of Crawford's body?' Soutar revealed an astonishing tale.

He claimed that while poaching in Crow Wood, near Dunecht House, late one night in late April or early May 1881, he was ambushed by two men. He made a run for it but was tripped up and pinned to the ground. His attackers, 'young-like chaps, of middle size' had their faces blackened. They spoke with an Aberdeenshire accent and seemed 'common'. As he lay sprawled on the ground they were joined by two masked accomplices. The new arrivals were of a different stamp. They appeared to be 'gentlemen', and spoke like educated men. Soutar claimed one of the men threatened him with a revolver at his breast. He said to his companion: 'Remove your arm, and I will settle him.' The other replied: 'It's all right. It's the rat-catcher. He's poaching.'

Soutar was told if he had been a spy he would have been shot, with the added threat: 'Remember what I am going to tell you; you're known to our party, and if you breathe a syllable of what you have seen, I will have your life if you're on the face of the earth.'

He was released but at daybreak he returned to the spot and found a man's body wrapped in a blanket. He thought he had uncovered a murder victim. The corpse smelled of benzoline and he believed efforts had been made to destroy it. Soutar refused to take police to the spot remarking: 'I'll rather wait until you get them that took the body; it will be safer for me then.'

Soutar's bizarre story was read out by the prosecution at his trial in the High Court in Edinburgh on Monday, 23 October 1882, when he was accused of violating the sepulchres of the dead and the raising and carrying away dead bodies out of their graves.

No witnesses were cited for the defence, and there was little or no cross-examination by the accused's counsel. But the Dean of Faculty did make one important point – the crime could not have been committed by Soutar alone, and therefore the mystery was only half-solved.

The Crown pin-pointed 27 or 28 May 1881 as the date of the outrage, as any earlier attempt would have been ruled out because of the severe winter of 1880-81. Soutar was spotted by several witnesses in the vicinity of Dunecht.

Witness James Collier, an Echt sawyer, recognised him on the Cluny coach from Aberdeen. He knew Soutar had recently been released from jail (in 1878 Soutar was imprisoned for 18 months for his involvement in a poaching incident which resulted in the death of a police sergeant). An innkeeper saw Soutar get off the coach and walk into the night. Where he went, what he did, or who else he met was unknown.

In his summing up to the jury at the end of the two-day trial, Lord Craighill, the presiding judge, agreed that it was 'perfectly impossible that one man alone could accomplish what had been done; probably more than two were concerned. The vault was opened and closed the same night without suspicion being aroused, and not only strength but skill was employed in the perpetration of this offence.'

The judge went on: 'The body was removed, the grave was dug, and all traces of these operations were obliterated. Probably these things were not all done on a single night, and certainly one man could not have done them; there must have been others. The guilt of the prisoner, however, if he were concerned, was in law the same as if he had been the sole offender.'

Soutar was found guilty and sentenced to five years' penal servitude. On his release from behind bars he continued to plead his innocence.

In 1883, Sheriff Guthrie Smith of Aberdeen considered

the claims of Machray, Philip and Collier, for the reward offered for information leading to Soutar's capture. The reward money was halved because it was considered Soutar was not the only villain. The £300 reward went to Machray. Collier accused the police of 'owlish stupidity' for not acting on his tip-off about meeting the accused on the Cluny coach.

The Dunecht Mystery endures. In the magazine, The *Deeside Field*, in 1929, E. R. Lumsden wrote: 'I happened to be driving from Cluny to Midmar by the Linton road which strikes the Tarland turnpike at Mill o' Hole, Midmar, and in the course of conversation with the driver, we got talking about the search for the Earl's body as we were passing woods that had at the time all been closely searched. After recalling the long searches throughout the district, the attempt to locate the body through clairvoyants, bloodhounds, etc., he remarked that the real outs and ins of the business were well-known to certain people in Echt at the time, and hinted that he had been himself given the chance of joining the venture.'

The Earl of Crawford's body was finally interred in the Lindsay family vault at Wigan after the town council gave special permission for the old vault to be reopened after a quarter of a century.

The Dowager, Lady Crawford, erected a small granite cross, protected by a fence, at the spot where her husband's body was found. The inscription records the theft and adds:-

He shall give his angels charge over thee
He that keepeth thee will not slumber

The heartless crime led to the advertising of the estate for sale in 1886. It was eventually sold in 1900 to A. C. Pirie of Craibstone. Lord Cowdray became the new owner before World War I. His biographer, J.A. Spender, has left an intriguing footnote to the outrage: 'Whatever spell the superstitious may have supposed to have been cast on the place by this incident was quickly broken by the cheerful Cowdray touch.'

The crypt at Dunecht House is no longer a sepulchre of

the dead. It now serves as a double garage, but there are still traces of the Victorian catacombs. The earl's coffin, a 'production' during the trial, was deposited in the vaults of old Parliament House in Edinburgh, now the Courts of Session.

Before the activities of grave-robbing faded into history and legend, it was unexpectedly resurrected on the brink of a new century. Horror gripped Victorian Scotland when a new scandal in Aberdeen resulted in black headlines. The *Pall Mall Gazette* observed: 'The body-snatching of an earlier day was scarcely equal to this.'

The *News of the World* growled: 'The reports from Aberdeen rival the stories of Burke and Hare in gruesome and horror. They indicate that no respect whatsoever has been paid to the sanctity of the tomb.'

And it warned: 'There is too much reason to fear that Aberdeen is not the only centre where such ghoulish performances take place, and the investigations may tend to reveal similar scandals in other places.'

The *Lancet* claimed the case had 'produced much mental disquietude among lairdholders, at least one of whom has died from excitement.'

Questions about the affair at Nellfield Cemetery were raised in Parliament.

In the summer of 1899, William Coutts, the cemetery superintendent, was arrested for the macabre events at the cemetery, within easy walking distance of the west end of Aberdeen's Union Street.

The scandal broke after the Harvey family sought interim interdict against the graveyard trustees, Aberdeen Baker Incorporation, and Coutts from interfering with their relatives' lair. A grave-digger with a grudge fingered Coutts who was accused of violating the sepulchres of the dead and perjury, the latter charge arising from the Harvey civil action.

A check of the graveyard revealed that scores of graves had been tampered with and the contents heartlessly exhumed and destroyed in most cases. The exhumation teams found decaying bodies crammed below footpaths.

Body-parts had been burned in the toolhouse furnace, and a pit contained 400 coffin handles and ashes. In one lair there had been 29 burials inside three months.

Coutts was no Victorian Burker. He had ordered his staff to empty lairs to create more internment space which could be resold. It also saved labour. For less earth had to be shifted than if a whole coffin had been buried.

His employers, of course, had been kept in the dark about his methods, and Coutts had not made a penny out of the cruel and heartless practice.

Coutts was locked up for six weeks in Craiginches Prison before he was allowed bail. This was for his own good, because the city was agog. In one evening thousands of people, some weeping and wearing black, visited the cemetery to gawk or check on a loved one's last resting place.

The factor of Nellfield Cemetery was mobbed by youths chanting, 'Burn the bodies!', and 'Nellfield Scandal', while his baker's shop in Chapel Street was boycotted.

When Coutts was smuggled out of jail a mob chased his coach, shouting: 'Nellfield pies!', which gives a hint of the sort of rumours sweeping Aberdeen.

The sordid scandal ended at Aberdeen High Court in September when on the fourth day of the trial Coutts changed his plea and was jailed for six months. Coutts was out of a job, but his employers had already picked his successor from 60 applicants from all over Britain.

Epilogue

The Resurrection Man is a historic bogeyman. But grave-robbing was not snuffed out overnight with the arrival of Warburton's Anatomy Act in 1832. The act repealed the law making the bodies of executed criminals available for dissection, although they could still be gibbeted, or buried within the precincts of the jail where they had been hanged. The act ensured the poorhouse would be the main source of dead bodies.

In June 1844 an attempt was made to lift the body of a child from the churchyard at Nairn. The grave-robbers – described as 'a band of ruffians' – were disturbed at their work when the deceased's relatives visited the grave in the evening. The four men fled, but the relatives mounted a watch the following night when the would-be bodysnatchers were again lurking in the area.

Harsh winters failed to stop the activities of the Aberdeen medical students during resurrectionist times. If a country road was blocked by snowdrifts lightning raids would be mounted by boat on the kirkyards within easy reach of the Dee and Don. It was said that 50 years after the passing of the Anatomy Act a group of 'medicals' rowed from Aberdeen to Peterculter to lift a body. The deed was carried out more as a dare, than in the name of science!

The bodysnatchers played a crucial role during the 18th and 19th centuries. Their labours, however abhorrent to the public at that time, advanced the cause of science.

In 1996, an Edinburgh theatre director and a Dundee playwright, working together on a play about the Edinburgh resurrectionists, were reported to feel so strongly about the bodysnatchers' service to science that they called for a permanent monument to be built in the city in their honour.

The memorials to the age of the bodysnatchers can still be seen in old graveyards: the watch-houses and watch-towers and those iron mort-safes that escaped being collected for scrap during World War Two. Coffin-shaped mort-safes were used as cattle water troughs on farms bordering the Aberdeenshire Dee. One enterprising farmer at Upper Mills, Crathes, built a wall across the middle of a mort-safe to serve two fields. He had bought the mort-safe from the kirk at Durris. It was eventually rescued from its ignominious role, and returned to the kirkyard.

One that served a similar purpose at nearby Maryculter was nicknamed, 'The Coffin'.

The macabre collection scattered around Scotland's medical schools and museums includes grislier items, such as Burke's skeleton and portions of his skin, tanned or tattooed, for posterity. Burke's cap of deerskin and leather, along with a fragment of his skin, are displayed in the Smith Art Gallery and Museum, Stirling. It was originally sold by a doctor in charge of Burke's body after his execution. Pieces of skin were also used to fashion a tobacco pouch, pocket book, card case and a wallet. A piece of skin bore the portraits of both Burkes and Hare!

In 1829, Madame Tussaud sent her talented son, Joseph, to Edinburgh to make a death mask of Burke and a plaster likeness of 'the infamous, the diabolical Hare' before his release from the Calton Jail. Their effigies were first exhibited in Liverpool in February 1829. Plaster heads of Burke and Hare are kept in the museums at the Royal College of Surgeons of Edinburgh and the University of Edinburgh.

Tanner's Close is no more but there is a pub in the West Port named after the infamous duo. Their fiendish exploits have been the subject of books, plays and movies.

The Museum of Scotland in Edinburgh has an interesting exhibit which may or may not be linked to the West Port Murders. Eight miniature wooden coffins, each containing a carved wooden figure, were part of a much larger collection found by boys in a small chamber on Arthur's Seat in 1836.

What was the purpose of the mysterious coffins and their strange occupants? Several explanations have been advanced over the years. One theory is that the dolls were used in witchcraft rituals.

The suggested association with the Burke and Hare

murders was put forward by Dr Sam Menefee and Dr Allen Simpson, in an article in the *Book of the Old Edinburgh Club*. There were apparently 17 coffins in the collection – exactly the number of bodies sold to Knox – but according to a contemporary newspaper report the boys destroyed the others during their horseplay.

So the Arthur's Seat coffins might represent a mock burial of the 12 women, three men, a youth and a boy whose bodies were bundled into tea-boxes or sacks by Burke and Hare and carted off to Surgeons' Square. When I inspected the dolls, snug in their coffins, a young visitor had left this message: 'These coffins are spooky. I wouldn't like to play with them even though they looked like children's toys.'

Mort cloths, shrouds, Victorian funereal jewellery, an old hearse, *memento mori* artefacts, and the sinister Airth mort-safe also remind visitors to the museums of their mortality.

Bibliography

Adams, Norman – Hangman's Brae (Banchory, 1993).

Baxter, Peter – Perth: Past and Present (Perth, 1928).

Black, Stewart – The Story of Paisley (Paisley, 1948).

Buchanan, William – Glimpses of Olden Days in Aberdeen (Aberdeen, 1870).

Christison, R. – The Life of Sir Robert Christison – Edited by his sons (Edinburgh, 1885).

Craig, James Whitelaw – Historical Notes on Paisley (Paisley, 1881).

Fleetwood, Dr John – The Irish Body Snatchers (Dublin, 1988).

Fraser, Duncan – Historic Fife (Perth, 1982).

Goodall, A.L. – Granville Sharp Pattison, the Argumentative Anatomist – The Scottish Society of the History of Medicine (Report of Proceedings, Session 1958-59).

Gordon, Anne – Death is for the Living (Edinburgh, 1984).

Hay, George – Architecture of Scottish Post-Reformation Churches (Oxford, 1957).

Henderson, John A. – Annals of Lower Deeside (Aberdeen, 1892).

Henderson, John A. – History of the Parish of Banchory-Devenick (Aberdeen, 1890).

Kelso, William – Sanitation in Paisley (Paisley, 1922).

Leighton, Alexander – The Court of Cacus (Edinburgh, 1861).

MacGregor, George – The History of Burke and Hare, and of the Resurrectionist Times (Glasgow, 1884).

Mackenzie, Peter – Old Reminiscences of Glasgow and the West of Scotland (Glasgow, 1890).

Martin, Andrew (compiler) – Scottish Endings: Writings on Death (Edinburgh, 1996).

Menefee, Samuel and Simpson, Allen – The West Port Murders and the miniature coffins from Arthur's Seat (Book of Old Edinburgh Club, New Series, Vol 3).

Moir, D.M. – The Life of Mansie Wauch, Tailor of Dalkeith; Written by Himself (Edinburgh 1905).

Pattison, F.L.M. – Granville Sharp Pattison; Anatomist and Antagonist 1791-1851 (Edinburgh, 1987).

Penny, George – Traditions of Perth (Perth, 1836).

Rae, Isobel – Knox the Anatomist (Edinburgh, 1964).

Ramsey, Ted – Don't Walk Down College Street (Glasgow, 1985).

Richardson, Ruth – Death, Dissection and the Destitute (London, 1987).

Riddell, John Scott – The Records of the Aberdeen Medico-Chirurgical Society (1789-1922) (Aberdeen, 1922).

Ritchie, James – Some Antiquities of Aberdeenshire and its Borders (Edinburgh, 1927).

Rodger, Ella Hill Burton – Aberdeen Doctors (Edinburgh, 1898).

Roughead, William – Twelve Scots Trials (Edinburgh & London, 1913).

Roughead, William – Trials of Burke and Hare (London, 1948).

Willsher, Betty – Understanding Scottish Graveyards (Edinburgh, 1995)

Wilson, William – Folklore and Genealogies of Uppermost Nithsdale (Dumfries, 1904).

Young, Alex F. – The Encyclopaedia of Scottish Executions 1750 to 1963 (Orpington, 1998).

Newspapers, periodicals etc:

Aberdeen Evening Express (1881-1882), Aberdeen Journal, Aberdeen Lancet, Aberdeen Magazine, Aberdeen Observor, Aberdeen University Review (1938-40), Caledonian Mercury, Dumfries Courier (1829), Edinburgh Evening Courant, Forres Gazette (1844), Glasgow Courant, Moray and Nairn Express (1885), Paisley Advertiser (1832), Proceedings of the Society of Antiquaries of Scotland (1911/12, 1920/21), The Scots Magazine (1742-1752).

Pamphlet entitled, Letter to the Lord Advocate etc by the Echo of Surgeons Square (1829) – Rare Books Division, National Library of Scotland.

Index